MANAGEMENT, SOCIAL WORK AND CHANGE

Management, Social Work and Change

Edited by

ELIZABETH HARLOW
University of Bradford, UK
JOHN LAWLER
Nuffield Institute, University of Leeds, UK

LONDON AND NEW YORK

First published 2000 by Ashgate Publishing

Reissued 2018 by Routledge
2 Park Square, Milton Park, Abingdon, Oxon OX14 4RN
711 Third Avenue, New York, NY 10017, USA

Routledge is an imprint of the Taylor & Francis Group, an informa business

Copyright © Elizabeth Harlow and John Lawler 2000

All rights reserved. No part of this book may be reprinted or reproduced or utilised in any form or by any electronic, mechanical, or other means, now known or hereafter invented, including photocopying and recording, or in any information storage or retrieval system, without permission in writing from the publishers.

Notice:
Product or corporate names may be trademarks or registered trademarks, and are used only for identification and explanation without intent to infringe.

Publisher's Note
The publisher has gone to great lengths to ensure the quality of this reprint but points out that some imperfections in the original copies may be apparent.

Disclaimer
The publisher has made every effort to trace copyright holders and welcomes correspondence from those they have been unable to contact.

A Library of Congress record exists under LC control number: 00132799

ISBN 13: 978-1-138-73385-5 (hbk)
ISBN 13: 978-1-138-73381-7 (pbk)
ISBN 13: 978-1-315-18749-5 (ebk)

Contents

	vii
List of Contributors	ix
Acknowledgements	

Preface: Management and Social Work: Do They Mix?   1
    Jeff Hearn

Introduction: Postmodernisation and Change in Social Work and   5
    Social Welfare
    Elizabeth Harlow

SECTION ONE   LOCAL PERSPECTIVES

1   From Beveridge to Best Value: Transitions in Welfare   19
      Provision
      Alan Siddall

2   The Rise of Managerialism in Social Work   33
      John Lawler

3   Developments in Services for Elderly People: Managing the   57
      Changes
      Kit Hall and Carol Jones

4   New Managerialism and Social Work: Changing Women's   73
      Work
      Elizabeth Harlow

5   Equalling the Opportunity of a Management Career   93
      Barbara Davey, Patricia Kearney and Gwen Rosen

SECTION TWO INTERNATIONAL PERSPECTIVES

6   Crossing, Building and Breaking the Boundaries: Social   119
    Work in a Global Context
    Liam Hughes

7   Managing the Development of Social Work in Russia   133
    Vladimir Kolkov, Boris Shapiro and Alexander Solovyov

8   Social Work Management in Finland   151
    Mikko Mäntysaari

9   In Search of Legitimacy: Social Work Management in Hong   167
    Kong
    Victor C. W. Wong and Sammy W.S. Chiu

    Conclusion: Emergent Themes   185
    John Lawler

List of Contributors

Sammy W.S. Chiu is Associate Professor at the Department of Social Work, Hong Kong Baptist University, China.

Barbara Davey is Research Fellow at the Research Unit, National Institute for Social Work, UK.

Kit Hall is Service Manager for older people with Nottingham Social Services Department, UK.

Elizabeth Harlow is Lecturer in Social Work, Department of Applied Social Sciences, University of Bradford, UK.

Jeff Hearn is Professorial Research Fellow at the University of Manchester and the Swedish School of Economics, Helsinki.

Liam Hughes is Director of Social Services for Bradford Social Services, UK.

Carol Jones is District Manager with Nottingham Social Services Department, UK.

Patricia Kearney is Director of Practice Development, Management Development Unit, National Institute for Social Work, UK.

Vladimir Kolkov is Professor of Social Policy and Social Work at the Institute of Youth, Moscow School of Social and Economic Sciences, Russia.

John Lawler is Lecturer in Leadership and Management at Nuffield Institute for Health, University of Leeds, UK.

Mikko Mäntysaari is Head of Research and Development at the National Centre for Welfare and Health, Finland.

Gwen Rosen is Consultant at the Management Development Unit, National Institute for Social Work, UK.

Boris Shapiro is Dean of the Faculty of Social Administration and Social Work at Moscow School of Social and Economic Sciences, Russia.

Alan Siddall is Assistant Programme Director in the England Programme of Save the Children UK.

Alexander Solovyov is Lecturer in the Faculty of Social Administration and Social Work at Moscow School of Social and Economic Sciences, Russia.

Victor C.W. Wong is Assistant Professor at the Department of Social Work, Hong Kong Baptist University, China.

Acknowledgements

A general expression of gratitude is offered to all secretarial and library staff at the University of Bradford who, in numerous and varied ways, have made contributions to the progress of this project. Thanks are particularly offered to Jean Hill and Sue Mackrill, secretaries in the Development and Project Planning Centre, University of Bradford, whose commitment to their work is beyond limit. Their willingness and efficiency has been crucial to the completion of the book: for their efforts we are most grateful. Appreciation is also extended to Jeff Hearn for his comments on the first draft of the book and the contribution of a preface. Finally, we would like to say thank you to all family and friends who have patiently supported us in our moments of frustration.

Preface: Management and Social Work: Do They Mix?

JEFF HEARN

'Management' is one of those words that often seems to evoke very contrasting reactions. For some, it is a dirty word; for others it is a panacea for all ills. In some cases these contrasting responses are held ambivalently by the same person or group of people. We may love and we may hate it. And when the talk turns from 'management' to 'managerialism', the responses tend to become yet more intense still. These contradictions apply all the more so to the meanings of management in and around social work. This is partly because at first sight management, or certain forms of management, appear to stand in tension with, and perhaps in opposition to, social work's traditional ethics concerning care and assistance. It can be argued that as managerialism has increased so have these tensions and ambivalences. In some senses then, we are living in 'different times', as argued in the Introduction to this book. Despite some postmodernist offerings to the contrary, such a postmodernist thesis and framework is itself an embedded historical reading.

Yet management may not be such a stranger to social work after all. In this sense some of the ambivalences around it, at least in the social work context, may not quite be what they seem. For a start, management has been there as part of social work from its modern beginnings. The Charity Organisation Society was clear about organisation and management. It was not just 'faith, hope and charity' but the organisation and management of charity on 'rational lines'. Indeed, social work requires some form of organisation. Social work is not just giving or helping; it is assistance located within the context of an agency or set of agencies. Without an agency, social work becomes something else – like being nice to your neighbour. In addition, agencies are not, at least very rarely, free-floating collectives in permanent revolution, but are themselves managed. The delivery of social work, whether directly or indirectly, needs managing, if only in the sense of gathering resources for the agency to continue to survive. That can be done by one person (the manager), several people (management), or everyone (managerial processes or self-management). Social work not only involves the ethic of care but also the imperative of control. For example, some residential, group care and family work is concerned with the control as well as the care of 'clients'. Management, in this context, can be seen as the higher order organisational control of day-to-day controls.

In recent years, political critiques in social work, and social work management have shared some principles – they have both been progressive, transformative and counter to tradition; they have both sought to develop welfare on a broad social policy scale rather than through individual casework; and in some senses they have been represented as optimistic, even youthful. This was evidenced even in the 1970s in the rather surprising links between radical social work of the 1970s and the rise of managerialism (Jones and Hearn, 1981). But the connection continues today with discussions of new forms of organisation, networking, inter-agency work, partnerships and collaborations, participations and empowerments.

There is a further paradox here in that more recently management has been associated with cutbacks, retrenchments and delayering. Whereas the general expansion of management has been associated with economic and organisational growth, much recent public sector managerialism has been characterised by decrementalism rather than incrementalism (Hearn and Roberts, 1976). This is a distinctive institutional phenomenon that has recurred during the oil crisis of the early 1970s, the neo-liberal restructurings of the 1980s and the early 1990s (Hearn and Small, 1984; Lawler and Hearn, 1995), and now the 'third way' of the 1990s. Some of these 'new public managements' are neo-Taylorist (Pollitt, 1990). In other cases they present more complex, flexible, mediated and value-based forms of management, concerned with quality and user-orientation (Newman and Clarke, 1994; White, 1999) – part of the movement from 'government' to 'governance' (Sotarauta, 1999). Hence, managerialist reforms (admittedly of different kinds) have been called upon not as part of the logic of expansion but to solve the problems of financial stringency. This has all happened when increased social difficulties might suggest a greater need of social work and social welfare.

Thus the central concern of this book – social work and management – is topical, timely yet intensely historical. Furthermore, and to be more specific, reading this book has brought to my mind several important and persistent themes. One I have already emphasised is the place of social work management in history. Another is the complex relationship of management and social work: is it social work management, social work and management, the management of social work, or perhaps social work/management? This takes us back, again historically, to long-running debates about the nature of the social work task. Third, there is the relation of social work to social services, social policy, and state welfare. Fourth is the question of organisational form and organisational change. This concerns the variable ways in which managers and management relate to wider organisational development. This includes the decline of the monolithic and monocultural bureaucracies, the creation of hybrid organisational designs, the impact of information technology, and the ubiquity of reorganisation. Fifth, the rise of management and managerialism in social work needs to be understood alongside social divisions, perhaps most obviously gender divisions but also other divisions, including those of age, class, ethnicity. Finally, on my list, is internationalism. It is very appropriate that international contributions – from Finland, Hong Kong and the Russian Federation – and international debates are central in this collection. It is important to realise that the British welfare system is not the only viable model and that state welfare provision dates from before 'Beveridge' in many countries. For example, in Finland governmental financial support to child care centres dates from 1913, and legislation on financial support to kindergartens and child care centres from 1923 (Tyyskä, 1995).

For all these reasons, this book needs to be read and discussed – not simply amongst the students of social work and social work management but amongst managers themselves. For while there is a growing literature of various types on social work management, much of this is either research studies of existing social work management practices or more prescriptive texts on how to do social work management. There have been fewer edited collections that have discussed the changing form of social work management within a broad international context. In doing just this, *Social Work, Management and Change* consolidates some old ground and breaks some new. Its contributors and editors have done social work and social workers a great service in extending the debate on the realities of this ever-present management. Equally importantly, they have also provided much needed material for the rethinking of management away from its own ever-present muse and inspiration – the world of business with its own special and specialist versions of economic and social life.

References

Hearn, J. and Roberts, I. (1976), 'Planning under difficulties: the move to decrementalism', in: K. Jones (ed.), *The Yearbook of Social Policy in Britain 1975*, Routledge and Kegan Paul, London.

Hearn, J. and Small, N. (1984), 'Planning the personal social services', in: C. Jones and J. Stevenson (eds), *The Yearbook of Social Policy in Britain 1983*, Routledge and Kegan Paul, London.

Jones, B. and Hearn, J. (1981), 'Radical social work and the problems of management', *Community Care*, no. 367, July, pp. 13-14.

Lawler, J. and Hearn, J. (1995), 'UK public sector organizations - the rise of managerialism and the impact of change on Social Service Departments', *International Journal of Public Sector Management*, vol. 8, no. 4, pp. 7-16.

Newman, J. and Clarke, J. (1994), 'Going about our business? The managerialization of public services', in: J. Clarke, A. Cochrane and E. McLaughlin (eds), *Managing Social Policy*, Sage, London.

Pollitt, C. (1990), *Managerialism and the Public Services*, Basil Blackwell, Oxford.

Sotarauta, M. (1999), 'The game of urban futures: what it takes to play in the network society', *Futura: Quarterly Magazine of the Finnish Society for Futures Studies*, vol. 18, no. 3, pp. 138-161.

Tyyskä, V. (1995), *The Politics of Caring and the Welfare State*, Suomalainen Tiedeakatemia, Helsinki.

White, S. (1999), 'Performing rationality: the limits of management in a social services department', in M. Dent, M. O'Neill and C. Bagley (eds), *Professions, New Public Management and the European Welfare State*, Staffordshire University Press, Stoke-on-Trent.

Introduction: Postmodernisation and Change in Social Work and Social Welfare

ELIZABETH HARLOW

This book brings to attention developments in social work and its management. In so doing it is by necessity multi-disciplinary: research and literature from the fields of management, organisation and social policy, as well as social work are drawn upon. The major theme of the book is change, which at the start of a new century, appears paradoxically, to be the major constant: that is, change is everywhere and living with change is part of the 'modern condition'. This is not to say that change has not always been a feature of life but the pace of change has, over recent time, increased dramatically. It is not only the speed of change but also the extent of change that is important. Theorists of postmodernisation are particularly concerned with exploring this phenomenon. Hence, their ideas are relevant as a contextualising framework to a book on management, social work and change.

For theorists holding to the postmodernisation thesis, every aspect of social life is being re-configured and this re-configuration has led to the dawning of a new historical era (O'Brien and Penna, 1998). This era marks a transition from modern society to a time when postmodernism proper will be fully established. This stage of postmodernisation involves an intensification of modernism, that is, an increase in rationalisation, differentiation and detraditionalisation. Organisations epitomize these processes and management is both a result of and a means by which they are achieved (Clegg, 1990). Given this, it is not a surprise that management as a practice and as a topic of interest has acquired such a high profile. However, the rise of managerialism and the nature of current change has to be understood within the context of four more general processes of postmodernisation. These processes are: political economic decentralisation; localisation; fragmentation; and desocietalisation

(O'Brien and Penna, 1998). There is no suggestion that these processes are consciously planned and implemented. On the contrary, they are the result of the complex interplay of politics, economics and culture. It is argued here that these processes are currently contributing either directly or indirectly to the reformation of social work organisation, management and practice. As a result, their influence is evident within the pages of this book. That is, as the various transformations of social work are articulated, their influence becomes apparent. Each process will constitute a theme around which the content of the book will be introduced. Although these processes are interdependent, each will be dealt with in turn.

Decentralisation

Dispersal

Decentralisation refers both to the vertical delegation of organisational power and its horizontal dispersal (Crook et al. 1992 cited in O'Brien and Penna, 1998). Siddall, in chapter one of this volume, focuses on developments in the UK and in so doing draws attention to the decline of the welfare state and the predominantly centralised provision of services. Although welfare provision, following the implementation of the Beveridge Report, was always meant to be pluralistic, state bureaucracies became the main providers of social care and social work services. This situation is now in the process of change and the authority to provide the range of welfare provision is being increasingly dispersed to both voluntary and private organisations.

The consensus over the state as the main provider of social services increasingly came into question when, following the oil crisis in the early 1970s, the post-war economic boom came to an end. Keynesian economic principles, the foundation upon which the welfare state depended, were seen as no longer valid. This coincided with the increased importance of global markets, the development of new methods of production, new technologies (particularly in telecommunications and computing) and the rise of neo-liberalism (Leonard, 1997). Proponents of neo-liberalism (such as Hayek, 1960 and 1967; Green, 1996) claim that a free market is the best means of delivering welfare. They argue that centralised systems lead to the destruction of individual freedom, individual responsibility and moral fortitude. The 'nanny state' was therefore seen as the root of many ills, including the erosion of enterprising, entrepreneurial activity by individuals. Such activity is crucial to a capitalist nation facing competition in an increasingly global marketplace.

Against this background of wider change, Leonard (1997) traces the rise of neo-liberalism from the late 1970s onwards. He argues that the collapse of the socialist critique, which intensified with the collapse of socialist countries in 1991, was significant. The significance was due to the (virtual) elimination of an alternative to the capitalist model of society and the principles of the free market. In addition, criticism of the welfare state had arisen from other sources: for example, feminists had argued that the welfare state was a reflection of the interests of the male ruling gender and, in consequence, perpetuated injustices and inequalities. Criticism also arose from those who considered large impersonal bureaucracies and centralised systems to be inefficient. This latter point is explored by Siddall who traces some of the criticisms and brings to attention the new role for voluntary and private organisations. However, he also questions whether what has become known as this new 'mixed economy of welfare' automatically brings improvement.

The 'mixed economy of welfare' is, therefore, a reflection of the dispersal of authority for the provision of services. However, as Siddall points out, the state continues to have a role in terms of encouraging, enabling and regulating the services provided. So, whilst neo-liberals might prefer a completely free market, the managed market is the current compromise (Adams, 1996). Within the UK, the management of the market involves centralised direction. The government achieves this by means of statute, guidance and circulars (Butcher, 1995) which constrain the practices of local authorities. To successfully create and manage the market at the local level, new organisational structures, roles, practices and skills have been required. A practical illustration of this is provided by Hall and Jones in chapter three. These authors describe the developments in services for older people in one particular authority following various governmental initiatives, including the introduction of the National Health Service and Community Care Act 1990 and the 1998 White Paper 'Modernising Social Services'. The chapter gives some indication of the almost continuous upheaval that has been experienced within Social Services Departments (SSDs) over recent years. Furthermore, it reveals the struggle in adapting to the neo-liberalist and market place philosophy which was to some extent at odds with the department's traditional commitment to the principles of the 'classic welfare state'.

As indicated above, in today's climate, management has assumed new enhanced status and importance. In the private sector management is thought to be the means by which companies can combat global competition: it is the means by which companies can get ahead and failing economies can be resuscitated. Indeed, according to Clarke and Newman (1993), managers have become today's super-heroes. It is not a surprise then, particularly given the ascendency of neo-liberalism, that approaches to management found within the private sector are thought to be relevant to the public sector. Using private sector knowledge and techniques, public sector managers are expected to introduce and maintain the mixed economy of welfare, and improve the economy, efficiency and effectiveness of services. The increasing importance of managers and private sector methods of management has been termed 'new managerialism'. The rise of new managerialism is the subject of chapter two. In this chapter Lawler introduces the term and scrutinises its impact on the public sector in general. There is some reflection upon its relevance and applicability before attention is turned to the consequences for social work organisations in particular.

This volume is not only concerned with developments in the UK. Chapters on social work in Russia, Finland and Hong Kong give testimony to the claim that change is a notable feature of modern life and all social work organisations. Furthermore, the postmodernising process of decentralisation - dispersal in particular - is evident. Given the transition from a communist regime to a Western style democracy, dispersal of authority is an important feature in Russian life in general. With regards to social welfare, voluntary organisations have assumed an increasingly important role as Kolkov, Shapiro and Solovyov, in chapter seven, discuss. This is partly accounted for by their responsibility for the dissemination of Western aid. Not only this, the increased activity is also a reflection of the developing role of social work. In Russia, social work as a profession is in its infancy, and debates about the delivery of social work services are influenced by developments in the UK as well as other Western countries. Hence, the work of voluntary, as well as commercial organisations is seen as a relevant addition to state run services. Consideration is being given to the introduction of internal markets in welfare but Kolkov *et al.* suggest that this may be too radical a move at this point in time. Whilst the introduction of a market in welfare might be seen by some as a positive way of encouraging competition and consumer choice, it is also resisted by many who favour a more traditionally Russian approach, and who resent the West's influence.

This latter sentiment is echoed by Mantysaari (chapter eight). Despite this, and concerns that the marketisation and privatisation of social work and welfare do not fit readily with Finnish tradition, they are being introduced in Finland. Voluntary agencies have for a long time been important providers of social work in Hong Kong which has had, and continues to have, only residual state services. However, as in the UK, managerialism is an increasingly important means by which the state regulates the nature of the services provided (see Wong and Chiu, chapter nine).

Delegation

Both Lawler in chapter two and Harlow in chapter four draw attention to claims that, in keeping with the postmodernisation thesis, power within social work organizations in the UK is being delegated to lower levels within the hierarchy. Indeed, it has been argued that managerial responsibility has been delegated as far as social workers themselves, who in turn are becoming managers of social work services rather than direct providers (Harris, 1998; Howe, 1996). However, in Finland, Hong Kong and the UK, delegated authority is tempered by the government's influence: organisational goals are set by the government and progress towards these goals is monitored. Where this brings about an improvement in social work services this may be beneficial. However, radicals (such as Dominelli, 1996) question whether such assumptions can be made: for radicals, delegation to social workers on these terms is little more than co-option to a project concerned with marginalising and controlling vulnerable individuals. Such a stance can be taken by neo-marxists or postmodernists, two sets of theorists who see the welfare system as concerned with the application of normative principles and, as such, inevitably contributing to the exclusion of certain groups within society (O'Brien and Penna, 1998). Whilst this text is not solely reflective of either of these theoretical frameworks, the work of critical theorists is drawn on as developments in social work are questioned and problematised.

Localisation

Intricately linked to the rejection of a centralised system of social welfare is the emphasis on services that are flexible and responsive to local need. Current thinking is that social work agencies should ascertain the needs of the local population and involve users in the design of services:

participation has become a buzz word. However, as Croft and Beresford (1990) point out, tensions underpin the notion of participation due to the competing principles upon which it is based. As a result of neo-liberal influence 'Listening to the public is seen as a way of helping service providers compete in the new market place of care' (Croft and Beresford, 1990, p. 8). At the same time, however, the notion of participation is a foundation stone of the politicised self-advocacy movement. Members of this movement are concerned with empowerment. Marginalised groups, such as disabled people, want to speak for themselves and gain greater control over their own lives. Hence, different notions of participation can be advocated by those concerned with empowerment politics and those concerned with the consumer's voice in the market place.

Critical commentators such as Adams (1998) indicate that recent developments in social work have given precedence to consumerism at the expense of empowerment. Both Lawler and Harlow (in this volume) refer to work of similar critics when they problematise new managerialism and its connection with consumerism. For example, Lawler asks whether social work service users can really be understood as consumers. Choice of services is limited and, given that they are relating to professional staff, they are less powerful than in other commercial exchanges. Drawing on the work of Dahlberg *et al.* (1999), Harlow questions the identity of consumers: are consumers past, present or future users and/or the people who pay taxes which (predominantly) fund the provision? Wong and Chiu (see chapter nine) highlight ways in which empowerment practice with service users is in jeopardy. As the government in Hong Kong attempts to regulate the work of voluntary agencies by means of grant allocation and service targets, opportunities for working in more radical ways become less likely. For instance, community development projects which may have facilitated marginalised groups in finding their own voice are being phased out. It appears that in Hong Kong also, consumerism is being given precedence over empowerment.

Despite the dominance of the consumerist discourse, concern with the empowerment of disabled people and black people, for example, continues along with other local politicised struggles. According to O'Brien and Penna (1998), local political struggle is another feature of postmodernisation. Activists rallying around a particular cause, such as animal rights or anti-road building, constitute a new form of resistance politics. New social movements are a part of this. However, the small scale focused nature of political projects does not mean that they are isolated from the global picture. On the contrary, postmodernisation also brings with it an awareness of the interdependence of localities that are geographically distant and local struggles can be part of global networks. For example, the movement concerning the empowerment of disabled people has worldwide connections (Croft and Beresford, 1990). Such connections can now be reinforced by means of recent advances in telecommunications.

In his discussion of globalisation, Hughes (in chapter six) gives attention to the interconnectedness of geographically distant localities. According to some theorists the autonomy of nation states is in decline as they are increasingly dependent on factors and events elsewhere in the world. For example, the rise of managerialism is said to result (in part) from the need to reduce welfare spending and compete more efficiently in global markets. Similar approaches to social policy and social welfare are seen to develop in response to common problems. In this volume, the rise of managerialism in social work is evident in Hong Kong and Finland. Furthermore, Russia's social work services are developing in accordance with Western influences. More explicitly, nations are uniting and developing similar policies, as in the European Union, for example.

Fragmentation

Decentralisation and localisation have led to the fragmentation of service provision. This theme is also evident in others areas that impact upon service provision. Political movements, for example, have also become fragmented as the analysis of injustice and oppression has evolved and brought with it different perspectives and demands for liberation. Universalism was an underlying principle of the welfare state. Although not an original goal, this appeared to herald a new equality (Lowe, 1994). Critics, however, soon began to highlight the way in which the welfare system perpetuated injustice and in the 1970s radical theorists (such as Corrigan and Leonard, 1978) exposed the oppressive aspects of social work. At this point most attention was given to class inequality. However, in the 1980s, attention became focussed upon injustices associated with 'race', ethnicity, disability, sexuality and gender. Universal needs and services became inceasingly in question as political groupings became mobilized around identity; the disabled people's self-advocacy movement noted above is an example of this.

The inclusion of two chapters on gender, social work and management is a reflection of the way in which concern for injustice has fragmented along the lines of identity. By drawing on the work of feminist theorists Harlow, in chapter four, argues that social work has traditionally been regarded as a feminine occupation. This is not only because the majority of practitioners are women, but because the tasks involved have reflected work carried out in the domestic domain. However, new managerialism is fundamentally changing the nature of social work and consideration is given to the implications for managers and practitioners. The second chapter reflecting feminist influences communicates the findings of empirical research carried out by the National Institute of Social Work (NISW). National studies on the workforce in personal social services carried out since 1992 have focussed on a) the differing career paths of men and women; b) job satisfaction and stress experienced by employees; and c) staff training and access to it (for example, see Ginn *et al.* 1997). Here, Davey, Kearney and Rosen report research findings on the differing career paths of men and women. At issue is the dominance of men within senior management. The research is contextualised in terms of explanations previously offered within the literature. Based on interviews with men and women staff in a number of SSDs, the authors conclude that the interest in becoming a manager is shared by both sexes. The issues which contribute to the likelihood of men being more successful are discussed in this chapter along with the ways in which change might be brought about.

The theme of fragmentation is also apparent in chapter six when Hughes explores the influence of postmodernism on social policy and social work. The main concern is that the attack on universalism has led to the inability to make claims about shared human need, common approaches to welfare or world-wide principles of social work. Furthermore, by rejecting the philosophy of the Enlightenment, postmodernism foregoes the notion of progress. For Hughes, the picture painted by postmodernists is bleak indeed and he notes, with some enthusiasm, the more optimistic approach of Doyal and Gough (1991). These authors retain the principles of universal humanity and believe that progress is possible. However, they acknowledge that human need and social work activity may be globally very varied.

Desocietalisation

The final characteristic of postmodernisation identified by O'Brien and Penna (1998) is desocietalisation. Once again this characteristic cannot be understood in isolation from decentralisation, localisation and fragmentation. For example, desocietalisation is in part a consequence of the fragmentation of nation states. The principle that a society is bounded territorially, culturally and politically has been undermined as states have disintegrated and national and social identities have become dispersed (O'Brien and Penna, 1998, p. 195). Yugoslavia and the Soviet Union are examples of the way in which nation states have fragmented. In addition, the boundaries of other countries, such as Ireland, are in dispute. Despite this fragmentation, the globalisation of communication and travel links localities in ways that were not previously possible. Migrants may cross boundaries of nation states but retain financial and social contact with their original location to such an extent that, 'it is clear neither which society is the home of migrants nor which social and economic networks comprise the society where exchanges and contacts occur' (O'Brien and Penna, 1998, p. 195).

In chapter six, Hughes discusses the movement of people across national boundaries. He draws attention to the differences that lead to migration. Whilst economic need may be a motivating factor, migrants may also be fleeing war or political persecution. Despite such unhappy circumstances, refugees and asylum seekers are not always well received. Within Europe they are offered some protected by the UN Convention on the Status of Refugees which prevents states from expelling them to a country where they risk persecution. However, in 1985 nine EU countries signed the Schengen Accord. Whilst this may have been a positive step towards the rationalisation of migration, border controls and visa requirements, it has also been criticized as an attempt to build 'Fortress Europe'. Within the European Union, each nation state has its own approach towards migrants. In some countries welfare services may be made available and citizenship restricted whilst elsewhere the opposite may be the case. In either situation, however, it is likely that migrants will find themselves at the social margins. Often accommodated in poor housing and, if employed at all, in low paid work. Marginalised people such as these are likely to turn to social work and social welfare services for assistance.

Concluding Comments and Structure of the Book

This introduction has attempted to locate recent changes in social work (including the rise of managerialism) within the wider processes of postmodernisation. Whilst not explicitly addressed in each chapter, these themes underpin much of the book's content. The more immediate concerns of each chapter are the day to day implications of the changes that are taking place. The overall goal is for the book to report and contribute to the debates which practically influence the working lives of managers and practitioners, and the services that are made available to those in need.

The book is divided into two parts: section one (chapters one to five) focuses on developments within the UK, whilst section two (chapters six to nine) has a global perspective. Chapter one introduces the general shift in the UK away from the 'classic welfare state' to the mixed economy of welfare. The rise of new managerialism is the specific focus of chapter two. Chapter three is a practical illustration of many of the changes that have been described. The experiences of one local authority transforming itself from the (predominantly) sole provider of services to its new role within the mixed economy are outlined. Gender and new managerialism are the topics of chapter four. At issue is the gendered nature of social work practice and management, and the appeal of each for future applicants. In addition, the declining emotional and analytical content of social work practice is highlighted. Chapter five reports on empirical research which investigated the over-representation of men in social work management.

Continuing to explore the topics of management, social work and change, the second part of the book takes a more international perspective. Chapter six has a crucial role because it elaborates the importance and consequences of globalisation. Thus, the connection between events in the UK and elsewhere are considered in detail. Chapters seven, eight and nine report on developments and topical issues in social work and social welfare in Russia, Finland and Hong Kong respectively. Each of these countries is experiencing significant social, economic and political change. For example, Russia is transforming itself from a totalitarian communist state to a democracy based on capitalist influences. Finland has recently joined the European Union and is making adjustments accordingly. Finally, Hong Kong is making the transition from being a British colony to a Special Administrative Region of China.

Each of these chapters briefly locates current social work within the region's history of providing welfare. As might be anticipated, there are major differences between each region's current provision (for example, social work in Russia is a new phenomenon). However, managerialist influences and commonalities are evident. Finally, the conclusion identifies and discusses the themes which have emerged in the preceding chapters. Whilst this introduction to the book argues that an identifiable set of trends are influencing the changes that are taking place, the conclusion highlights the contradictory, and even paradoxical outcomes that have been described.

References

Adams, R. (1996), *The Personal Social Services*, Longman, Harlow.
Adams, R. (1998), *Quality Social Work*, Macmillan, Basingstoke.
Butcher, T. (1995), *Delivering Welfare. The Governance of the Social Services in the 1990s*, Open University Press, Buckingham.
Clarke, J. and Newman, J. (1993), 'The Right to Manage: a Second Managerial Revolution?', *Cultural Studies*, vol. 7, no. 3, pp. 427-41.
Clegg, S.R. (1990), *Modern Organizations. Organization Studies in the Postmodern World*, Sage, London.
Corrigan, P. and Leonard, P. (1978), *Social Work under Capitalism*, Macmillan, Basingstoke.
Croft, S. and Beresford, P. (1990), *From Paternalism to Participation. Involving People in Social Services*, Open Services Project/Joseph Rowntree Foundation, London.
Crook, S., Pakulski, J. and Waters, M. (1992), *Change in Advanced Society*, Sage, London.
Dahlberg, G., Moss, P. and Pence, A. (1999), *Beyond Quality in Early Childhood Education and Care: Postmodern Perspectives*, Falmer Press, London.
Dominelli, L. (1996), 'De-professionalizing Social Work: Anti-oppressive Practice, Competencies and Postmodernism', *British Journal of Social Work*, vol. 26, pp. 153-75.
Doyal, L. and Gough, I. (1991), *A Theory of Human Need*, Macmillan, Basingstoke.
Ginn, J., McLean, J., Andrew, T. and Balloch, S. (1997), *Work Histories of Social Services Staff*, NISW, London.
Green, D.G. (1996), *Community Without Politics. A Market Approach to Welfare Reform*, Choice in Welfare Series No. 27, IEA, London.
Harris, J. (1998), 'Scientific Management, Bureau-Professionalism, New Managerialism: The Labour Process of State Social Work', *British Journal of Social Work*, vol. 28, pp. 839-62.
Hayek, F.A. (1960), *The Constitution of Liberty*, Routledge and Kegan Paul, London.
Hayek, F.A. (1967), *New Studies in Philosophy, Politics and Economics*, Routledge and Kegan Paul, London.
Howe, D. (1996), 'Surface and Depth in Social Work Practice', in N. Parton, (ed), *Social Theory, Social Change and Social Work*, Routledge, London.
Leonard, P. (1997), *Postmodern Welfare. Reconstructing an Emancipatory Project*, Sage, London.
Lowe, R. (1994), 'Lessons from the Past: the Rise and Fall of the Classic Welfare State in Britain, 1945-76', in A. Oakley and A.S. Williams, (eds), *The Politics of the Welfare State*, UCL Press, London.
O'Brien, M. and Penna, S. (1998), *Theorising Welfare: Enlightenment and Modern Society*, Sage, London.

SECTION ONE

LOCAL PERSPECTIVES

1 From Beveridge to Best Value: Transitions in Welfare Provision

ALAN SIDDALL

Introduction

The purpose of this chapter is to locate the management of social work within the context of the change which has been taking place in the provision of welfare services since the end of the Second World War. In particular, the chapter will examine the developing relationship between different providers of welfare, the balance between statutory and non-statutory provision and the increasing role of the independent sector. The development of state welfare and social work is briefly considered in order to contextualise current and future pressures on social work managers. A newcomer to social work at the turn of the millennium could be forgiven for thinking that contracts and partnership agreements, tendering and purchasing have always been fundamental to welfare provision. However, these concepts are relatively new and the job of a service manager has altered considerably.

Introduction and Development of the Welfare State

The welfare state in the UK is generally seen as being established by the Labour government immediately after the Second World War (Johnson, 1987). The major blueprint for the policies was the Beveridge Report of 1942. Following many of the recommendations, the Atlee administration clearly placed the state as the major provider of welfare services which included social security, health, housing, education and personal social services. Under the Keynesian approach of the time, fundamental to the aims of the welfare state was the economic and social goal of full employment. This would provide sufficient tax revenues to fund such services but perhaps more importantly; it would provide people with a route away from poverty through paid work.

In the immediate post-war atmosphere there was a strong feeling that the time had come for the state to play the central role in comprehensive health and welfare provision: the state would replace the fragmented and partial pre-war arrangements. The overall mood reflected the desire to avoid a return to the difficulties of the severe pre-war economic conditions or to the health and welfare inequalities which had characterised the early years of the century. There was a new consensus: right-wing politicians believed that the state had a central role to play within a capitalist framework and left-wing politicians accepted a mixed economy of welfare, though emphasising a central state role in both planning and provision. Whilst this new state role in welfare was accepted, decisions remained over the implementation of policies, particularly how the resulting services would be delivered. The market was not seen as being able to provide the necessary mechanisms. This previous failure of unregulated markets to provide for common welfare is often overlooked in the development of UK welfare (Barr, 1987, in Lowe, 1994). In addition, whilst there was a history of voluntary welfare provision throughout the 1800s and early 1900s, this was seen as being diverse and uncoordinated. The government of the time chose to follow the path of state welfare in both defining policy and delivering services. Brenton (1985) rightly suggests that this central role for the state was not inevitable. The state could have chosen to finance and regulate the voluntary sector as its agent, as happened in the United States and The Netherlands, or it could have decided to refocus on the operation of markets. However, the market was not seen as an appropriate provider of welfare services and was largely ignored. The voluntary sector was not directly regulated out of existence but was expected to wither away. Thus, the Labour government chose to invest in statutory services as a means of promoting comprehensive and universal provision.

From this time, the welfare state infrastructure began to develop and continued over the next three decades. Butcher (1995) usefully charts the development of the welfare state and sees it as having three distinct phases. The first, from 1945-1976, was one of development but relative consensual stability. The much shorter period from 1976-1979 was a time of welfare provision being under specific financial strain and from 1979 to 1995 as undergoing radical reassessment. Powell and Hewitt (1998) and

Rao (1996) highlight that, whilst the 1945-1976 period is often described as a period of major consensus, there were significant dissenting voices to the central role of government in both economic and social domains. However, this was a period of relative growth and political stability. Relationships were strong between a central government dealing with the 'high' political issues (Lowe, 1994) of macro-economics and social policy and local government largely responsible for delivering welfare services. The voluntary and independent sectors continued to exist however. The state was not to become a monopoly provider of welfare services. The relative slow pace of development of statutory services in the 1950s helped voluntary organisations maintain their position in welfare provision, and gave them time to review their role. Furthermore, Government reports (Nathan Committee, 1952; Younghusband Committee, 1959) in the 1950s were positive about voluntary organisations and their contribution to welfare provision was encouraged. Whilst this period to 1976 was relatively stable, there were, nonetheless, changes in thinking on welfare and changes to its organisation and management, particularly in relation to social work. There was still a consensus on the role of the state as a major provider of welfare, but already it could be seen that an entire state monopoly of welfare was unsustainable due to the increasing demand on services together with finite state resources. The voluntary sector was acknowledged as providing valuable welfare service support.

As services and legislation developed, problems of organisation and co-ordination also grew. The Seebohm Report (1968) recommended a new structure for social work services. New departments would replace the old welfare and children's departments, and participation of local people and consumers was to be encouraged. The state, through local authorities, was still seen as being prime provider of social work services but by the time the report was published, the continued role of voluntary organisations as a supplement to a strong framework was clear. In highlighting resource limitations for state provision, Seebohm looked towards using community resources to augment state provision. The concept of 'partnership' was developing.

The period from 1976 to 1979, whilst much shorter than that discussed above, can be seen as a major transitional period both in political and social policy terms. During this period, the state could not sustain its general levels of expenditure, including its welfare expenditure. In addition, any hope of full employment, a fundamental requisite for many in achieving a welfare state, was deemed unrealistic. The oil crisis at this time added to concerns regarding expenditure on welfare provision. Whilst attempting to maintain core welfare services within the state sector, governments of different political flavours implemented cuts in public spending. Attempts made to reduce public expenditure during this period was largely based on persuasion rather than coercion. Governments were concerned with total levels of expenditure rather than with spending on a more localised basis (Butcher, 1995). However, even a 'no-growth' welfare state was proving difficult to finance and, to keep up with increasing demands, new sources of support were felt to be necessary. The Conservative Party, which was to form the government from 1979, looked both to its traditions of support for philanthropy and charity and to newer monetarist philosophy as the way forward. The relative consensus born in the late 1940s and sustained, albeit in modified form, for the next three decades was to give way by the end of this period to a new radicalism of the political right.

The development of this 'new right' philosophy saw voluntary organisations and the independent sector beginning to be represented as integral to welfare provision rather than as complementary to it. The Friedmanite monetarist philosophy of the new right saw public spending as a millstone around the neck of wealth creation which should be reduced to minimal levels. The growing demands on welfare services, exacerbated to a significant extent both by an increasing elderly population and by high levels of inflation, were understood to pose a threat to economic growth. The encouragement of self-help, voluntary and commercial provision was seen as the means of maintaining welfare without increasing the burden on the state. Such an economic philosophy did not stand in isolation. It was part of an overall philosophical approach which viewed the role of the centralised state as negative but which was also reluctant to delegate significantly to local government, much of which was seen as having quite a different agenda. The 1980s saw the promotion of individual freedom and responsibility. This implied a minimal state with a role confined to regulatory functions.

Concern with expenditure levels at this time became focused at the level of local government. There was considerable ideological disagreement between central and local government, the result of which was the elevation of local government to the arena of 'high', i.e. national, politics (Lowe, 1994). The impact on welfare services was that now local authorities were being forced by financial and legislative constraints to accept a role as providers solely of basic services, focused on areas for which they had statutory responsibility. Experimentation and innovation became luxuries for many local authorities. Instead, the pioneering qualities of voluntary organisations and entrepreneurial spirit of the independent sector was increasingly recognised as ways of enabling and developing services beyond the mainstream. This was in keeping with the new right principle that individuals should become less reliant on the state in general and take more responsibility for their own welfare provision. Hence, whilst provision by the state was still significant, the informal sector was important in a continuing focus on individual 'self-help'. The Conservative Manifesto of 1979 was to urge that:

> We must do more to help people to help themselves to look after their own. We must also encourage the voluntary movement and self-help groups working in partnership with statutory services (quoted in Brenton, 1985, p. 25).

Self help was seen to be an integral element of citizenship. Home Office Minister Patten in 1988 described his concept of the 'active citizen' as 'someone making more than a solely economic contribution to his or her community' (quoted in Holman, 1988). In analysing the content of Patten's argument, Holman suggests that the 'active citizen' was being presented as one who becomes increasingly involved in voluntary activity as her or his affluence and leisure time increases. Holman points out that one's contribution in the community is never 'solely economic' and that a mass of 'active citizenship' exists already, traditionally in very poor areas. However, he concluded that poverty limits active citizenship and that 'government action to redistribute goods and powers more fairly throughout society is the prerequisite for all citizens to participate in voluntary movements' (Holman, 1988, p. 17). Government though, did not share these views.

The Conservative governments of the 1980s and 1990s held to the assertion of their 1979 Manifesto that 'in the community, we must do more to help people to help themselves and the family to look after their own. We must also encourage the voluntary movement and self help groups acting in partnership with the statutory services' (Conservative Party Manifesto quoted in Brenton, 1985, p. 51). This was entirely consistent with a 'help yourself' attitude to finding your own work, starting your own business, taking out your own pension, and insuring your own health. It ran parallel to talk of the 'Nanny State' and derision of public services which changed the public's perception of state provision. Conservative Ministers continued to make their support for this position clear. By the late 1980s statutory organizations were no longer primary providers, simply complemented by voluntary activity. They had been persuaded, or in some cases coerced, into encouraging the development of voluntary and independent organizations. Latterly they were seen as playing a tertiary role, alongside the voluntary and commercial sectors, of supporting 'self-help' and active citizenship.

Private service provision has existed for some time in welfare, for example, in nursing care. The extent of such provision, however, has previously been relatively small scale. The policies of Conservative governments from 1979 actively promoted an increase in this system of care. Throughout the 1980s there was considerable debate about the policy of privatising a wide range of public sector organisations and activities. However, the debate over private provision of welfare was less heated. Whilst suggesting that 'welfare policies constitute a major divide between the political parties', in a subsequent analysis of the respective party manifestos of 1987, Papadakis and Taylor-Gooby concluded that:

> Conflicts over welfare denationalisation have become less marked than those over the privatisation of state-owned industries. The place of private services in welfare is not seriously challenged by any of the main parties (Papadakis and Taylor-Gooby, 1987, p. 14).

In attacking dependence on state welfare provision, the Conservative government generated policies which created an atmosphere both nationally and locally which supported a transfer of resources and responsibilities. They introduced the most radical set of legislative changes since the 1940s and perhaps at any time this century. These were based on a view of local government as negative; 'usually based on its attitude towards a small handful of Labour authorities' (Gutch and Young, 1988, p. 10). This led to a further diminution of the state's role in providing services directly and to services being provided increasingly by private, voluntary and informal sources. Thus, we can see that during this time there was a developmental trend away from state provision, an increasing reliance on the role of the individual and of self-help, and the development of a stronger independent, commercial sector within welfare. This trend signified a revised view of the role of local authorities in providing welfare services.

Changing Role of Local Government

As noted above, from 1979 significant changes to policy and finances for and within local government were introduced, together with an increasing emphasis on the use of voluntary and commercial organisations in welfare provision. The consequences for local government of national policies could be summarised as: imposing strict limits on spending, changing their systems of accountability and changing their roles and responsibilities. In the 1980s and early 1990s reductions in the rate support grant, financial penalties and rate capping all had a significant effect on the way local authorities were able and allowed to operate (Butcher, 1995). The introduction of the poll tax, later to become the council tax, incurred costs for local authorities, reduced income from industry in areas already encountering economic decline and led to a further control of spending and reduction in local autonomy. Furthermore, these changes in the local rating system affected the accountability of the local authority to local people. Legislation to abolish the Greater London Council and Metropolitan County Councils not only changed the management of some services in these areas but introduced non-elected appointees to oversee the change. This action in itself highlights the lack of confidence of the government of the day in locally elected members and the tension between national government and some local authorities at the time. Many of the functions of local government were devolved to others. The establishment of Health Trusts, Housing Action Trusts, and independently funded colleges and polytechnics, together with 'opted out' schools, increased power of school governors and enforced competitive tendering are amongst the measures introduced in this period. Regarding social services provision in particular, the recommendations of the Griffiths Report (1988) on community care had substantial implications for local government. These recommendations led to an increase in contracted out services. This significant report also provided an ideological link between the past and the future. It harked back to welfare ideologies of the past in terms of stimulating community action, whilst simultaneously presaging the future by influencing local authorities to purchase services from other providers (Butcher, 1995) and encouraging them to become 'enablers' rather than providers. This new role was reinforced further by important legislation affecting social work, most notably, the Children Act (1989) and the NHS and Community Care Act (1990).

The impact of policies such as these was to define more clearly the role of social work and to enable the further development of markets in care. The roles of social workers came under increasing scrutiny, for example, in terms of child care, social workers became more accountable to the courts in the exercise of statutory powers. It was at this time the role of managers in social work was particularly strengthened:

> community care reforms envisaged key roles for senior 'strategic' managers and for care managers, squeezing out superfluous intermediaries. It was up to senior managers to take the lead in deciding strategy, planning change, taking stock of resources, defining and measuring local needs and establishing priorities and targets (Langan, 1998, p. 166).

This new role for managers in social care was part of a general rise in managerialism throughout the public sector. The new role was reinforced by the delegation of greater powers to managers. Also the language and mechanisms of managerialism were adopted in preference to the professional modes of operating which had previously prevailed. The resulting trend represents very different roles from those envisaged at the institution of the welfare state: different roles for national and local government; for professionals and managers; emphasis on different mechanisms, market mechanisms, for delivering social care; and a different status for 'consumers' rather than 'clients'. In addition to changes in roles there have also been shifts in mechanisms for delivery and in the language of welfare. Examples of these shifts include change: from assessment of need to consumer demand; from state provision to increasing provision by voluntary and private sectors; from acceptance of existing standards of service to the need to promote quality; and from state direction of welfare to partnerships. The situation now is one where the mixed economy of care is accepted as a legitimate, institutionalised approach to social services provision.

The growing role of the independent sector in this mixed economy is seen as important in enhancing efficiency and ensuring quality and choice. However, evidence of the impact, or operation in practice, of wider consumer choice, increased quality of service or greater user involvement is still sparse, in spite of a growing independent sector in many areas of social care. Langan (1998) in particular questions the results of this restructuring and redefinition of management and of social work provision. The commercial sector is seen by many as substantively different from both the statutory and voluntary sectors. Whilst some compatibility is recognised between state and voluntary providers in respect of some coincidence of values, concepts such as consumer demand and profit within social work remain problematic. The position of private welfare service provision is a still controversial and relationships across sectors need to be managed sensitively. Whilst the central role of the consumer or user is seen as a prime element for all welfare providers, issues of accountability, power and transparency are still unclear (Loney et al., 1991). These issues present challenges to managers of social work in ensuring the most appropriate packages of care are identified and delivered and that the ethical values of social work are being upheld in a quasi-market context. The Labour Government, elected in 1997, has continued the policies of mixed welfare economy. In many respects this is difficult to evaluate yet. Policies on health and social work provision have abounded since the government took office. The impact of these is considered next.

Recent Developments and Implications

Recent government initiatives prove well the adage 'change is the only constant'. It is very difficult to predict the longer term impact of rapid and complex policy change, though it is safe to say that we are not witnessing a significant reversal of the policies of the preceding government. This conversion of the left to the philosophies of the right has not escaped notice and comment (for example, Cutler and Waine, 1994). Some commentators (for example, Ellison and Pierson, 1998) note aspects both of continuity with, and change from, previous government policies: change, in the form of a new awareness of issues such as feminism, antiracism and ecology and a focus on 'inclusion'; continuity, in the state's central role in social policy strategy but not its delivery. We may have seen some change and some repackaging but the many new government initiatives do not signify a move away from the management and market trends established earlier. These current initiatives all continue to have considerable implications for managers within social work. The current tide of guidance, advice and policy expansion affecting local government and their social services departments include:

- Modernising Social Services (DofH, 1998), promoting independence and higher quality services;
- a move towards combination of health care and social care, especially primary health care;
- the introduction of Quality Protects requirements for the protection of children looked after by local authorities;
- the development of Youth Justice Boards and Young Offenders Teams which require increased multi-disciplinary working;
- a Royal Commission on long term care, with potential implications for inter-organisational working;
- developments in mental health, including compulsory treatment orders and increased pressure for community safety;
- The introduction of 'Best Value', the aim of which is to optimise a combination of cost-effectiveness and high quality standards.

All the above are likely to affect relationships between different agencies significantly, stimulating a review of relationships and actively encouraging partnership arrangements in social care provision. The Best Value concept particularly, is central to the White Paper on Local Government (DofETR, 1998). It includes a duty to consult and engage with communities; the introduction of 'Beacon Councils' and National Standards; a requirement to seek competition in promoting services and to set targets for continuous improvement. The White Paper also includes the development of Standards Boards, scraps the idea of 'capping' of budgets (though retains powers to intervene) and introduces options for local decision-making processes. Local Performance Plans will include joint working arrangements with partners and will be reviewed every five years. Authorities are urged to challenge, compare, consult and compete. This follows a pattern, seen also in health and education, for the publication of centralised performance measures. The trend is for greater transparency and greater accountability, delivered largely through managerialist means, and is a very different process from that envisaged in the infancy of the welfare state. We thus have seen very significant changes since that time: from initial aspirations of state-run universalist provision delivered through professional services in a context of full employment, to a pragmatic, pluralist welfare structure, with increasing selectivity and targeting of services and with managers in key co-ordinating roles. Arrangements between all respective agencies in welfare have altered:

> relationships between statutory, private, voluntary and informal provision have changed both organisational boundaries, (joint working, strategic partnership and contracting) and undermined distinctions between previously differentiated workforces (Clarke et al., 1994, p. 228).

Expectations on managers are high. They will need well developed management skills to fulfil those expectations, both in co-ordinating services within organisations and in working across organisational boundaries. Whilst increasing partnership arrangements between different organisations within social work provision will be one direct outcome of such initiatives, the outcome of changes at the organisational level is less certain. Parston (1998) feels that a clearer vision is needed at the level of individual organisations. Managers will need to 'keep the visionary message alive...their job is to drive change...to enable those on the ground to understand clearly, to make judgements, to innovate and to design local changes that they know intuitively to be right' (Parston, 1998, p. 96). Not only do they need to provide vision and leadership, there are further, idealised and unrealistic expectations placed on managers in social work. Langan and Clarke (1994) state that management is seen by many as:

> the alchemist's stone which will transform a leaden and costly bureau-professional organisation into a flexible and efficient one. For those inside the mixed economy of care, the debate about optimistic or pessimistic prognostications over whether this magic will work is somehow beside the point. They now inhabit a world whose basic elements have been transformed – the structures, cultures, languages and practices are different and the old elements cannot be recovered. The ground has changed under them and the issue is how to mange to survive In the new world. This 'cultural revolution' captures precisely the magic of mangement: the ability to recastold assumptions and patterns into a new configuration which promises happy endings (Langan and Clarke, 1994, p. 90).

How the role of social work manger has changed since the introduction of Social Services Departments! A manger then would be judged on her/his ability to relate to 'clients', knowledge of casework methods and of relevant legislation. Line managers of social workers were usually senior social workers; that is, they were practising social workers with additional administrative and supervisory responsibility. A significant task for social work managers now is to manage the expectations of those experiencing and evaluating their work. The expectations of new public management may be very considerable, as noted above. Managers are currently concerned, and will increasingly be concerned with managing relationships between their agency and a range of other agencies and interest groups, and juggling interests of their teams, their organisations and their partners. They will be trying to meet targets, maintain standards and trying to ensure that they can explain their actions. They will need to know how to consult with others, including 'the community', and to understand how to assess and interpret outcomes. They will need to understand issues of organisational culture in order to promote the necessary organisational change to ensure best use of partnership relationships. They will need to know how to manage inter-disciplinary teams and workers who see things differently from them. They will need to be politically astute to make best use of the politics of their area and region. They will need to manage resources and know how to secure them. They will need to ensure that service users get what they need. They will have to be adept at the management of change.

References

Barr, N. (1987), *The Economics of the Welfare State*, Weidenfeld and Nicholson, London.
Beveridge, W.H. (1942), *Social Insurance and Allied Services*, Cmnd 6404, HMSO, London.
Breton, M. (1995), *The Voluntary Sector in British Social Services*, Longman, London.
Butcher, T. (1995), *Delivering Welfare: The Governance of the Social Services in the 1990s*, Open University Press, Buckingham.
Clarke, J., Cochrane, A. and McLaughlin, E. (1994), 'Mission Accomplished or Unfinished Business? The Impact of Managerialism', in J. Clarke, A. Cochrane and E. McLaughlin (eds), *Managing Social Policy*, London, Sage.
Cutler, T. and Waine, B. (1994), *Managing the Welfare State*, Berg, Oxford.
DofETR (Department of Environment, Transport and the Regions) (1998), *Modern Local Government: In Touch with the People*, Cmnd 4041, HMSO, London.
DofH (Department of Health) (1998), *Modernising Social Services*, Report prepared by the Secretary of State for Health Cm4169, The Stationery Office, London.
DHSS (Department of Health and Social Security) (1989), *Caring for People: Community Care in the Next Decade and Beyond*, Report prepared by the Secretary of State for Health and Social Security, HMSO, London.

Ellison, N. and Pierson, C. (1998), 'Conclusion' in N. Ellison and C. Pierson (eds), *Developments in British Social Policy*, Macmillan, Basingstoke.
Griffiths, R. (1988), *Community Care: Agenda for Action A Report to the Secretary of State for Social Services*, HMSO, London.
Gutch, R. and Young, K. (1988), *Partners or Rivals?*, LGTB, Luton.
Holman, B. (1988), 'Give me the Tools', *Community Care*, 24th Nov, pp. 16-17.
Johnson, N. (1987), *The Welfare State in Transition: Theory and Practise of Welfare Pluralism*, Wheatsheaf, Brighton.
Langan, M. (1998), 'The Personal Social Services' in N. Ellison and C. Pierson (eds) *Developments in British Social Policy*, Macmillan, Basingstoke.
Langan, M. and Clarke, J. (1994), 'Managing in the Mixed Economy of Care' in J. Clarke, A. Cochrane and E. McLaughlin (eds), *Managing Social Policy*, Sage, London.
Loney, M., Boocock, R., Clarke, J., Cochrane, A., Graham, P. and Wilson, M. (1991), *The State or the Market: politics and welfare in contemporary Britain*, 2nd edition, Sage, London.
Lowe, R. (1994), 'Lessons from the Past: the Rise and Fall of the Classic Welfare State in Britain, 1945-1976', in A.Oakley and A. Susan Williams (eds), *The Politics of the Welfare State*, UCL Press, London.
Nathan Committee (1952), *Report to the Committee on Law and Practice Relating to Charitable Trusts*, Cmnd 8710, HMSO, London.
Papadakis, E. and Taylor-Gooby, P. (1987), *The Provision of Public Welfare*, Wheatsheaf, Brighton.
Parston, G. (1998), 'Outcomes and the Clarity of Vision', *The Stakeholder*, vol. 2, no. 4, pp. 7-9.
Powell, M. and Hewitt, M. (1998), 'The End of the Welfare State?', *Social Policy and Administration*, vol. 32, no. 1, pp. 1-13.
Rao, N. (1996), *Towards Welfare Pluralism: Public Services in Times of Change*, Dartmouth, Aldershot.
Seebohm, F. (1968), *Local Authority and Allied Personal Social Services*, Cmnd 3703, HMSO, London.
Younghusband Committee (1959), *Report of the Working Party on Social Workers in Local Authority Health and Welfare Services*, HMSO, London.

2 The Rise of Managerialism in Social Work

JOHN LAWLER

Introduction

Since the late 1970s public sector organisations have come under considerable scrutiny: much change has been introduced. As a result of privatisation, many organisations which formed part of this sector no longer do so. Those which remain in this sector have altered in many ways as their purposes and characteristics have been analysed and redefined. This chapter looks in detail at aspects of those changes. The interpretation and development of managerialism is discussed together with the impact of managerialism across the public sector in general. Services for health, housing and education, for example, are all affected by these developments. Having considered the general context of public sector organisations, the impact on social work organisations specifically is then discussed.

What is 'Managerialism'?

Major changes have affected public sector organisations in many different countries over the last two decades. Two important influences on these organisations have been, firstly, the effects of the privatisation of many such organisations or parts of them and, secondly, the rise of managerialism within those which remain in the public sector. Managerialism refers to the development of the interests of management, as opposed to any other function or position in the organisation. This development stresses the role, power and accountability of individual managers and accentuates their positions as managers rather than as administrators, officers or senior professionals. Accountability for success or otherwise lies at the door of each individual manager, operating within strategic guidelines and being responsible for the achievement of organisational objectives.

The essence of managerialism is the belief that the managerial processes of many organisations have a great deal in common, be they public or private sector and, as such, people equipped as managers should be able to operate effectively in any domain. There is, therefore, a belief in the transferability of these skills to other managerial contexts.

> The managerialist ethos which has developed is based on the view that managers have 'the right to manage', which means that they should be in control of the organisations which they run and they should be very proactive.... It is this view of managers as controllers which underlies many of the managerial reforms in the public sector. Administering systems which are in a steady state, and doing so by arriving at a consensus among managers of various departments and with trade unions is not considered to be real 'management'.... Part of the managerial ideology is that there is no difference between running a factory and running a hospital (Flynn, 1990, p. 177-8).

This assumption, that the transfer of management practices from one sector to another, is one which is open to challenge and which will be discussed in due course. The view that managerialism, or the 'managerial ethos' noted above, can be seen from one agreed perspective is also open to challenge. Certainly, managerialism is seen as having a number of prime facets which distinguish it from previous modes of administration:

> [It] places emphasis on policy management and implementation rather than on policy development and design in public administration; stresses efficiency, effectiveness and quality, as against process and equity in the management of public resources; ... advocates the use of private-sector management practices in the public sector; seeks to diffuse responsibility and to devolve authority;... shifts the public accountability focus from inputs and processes to outputs and outcomes and prefers to create wherever possible a competitive public administration (Dixon *et al.*, 1998, p. 168-9).

The main characteristic can be seen as authority for the successful operation of the organisation now lying with managers (Keen and Scase, 1996). This development indeed established the role of managers and gave them the 'right to manage' (Pollitt, 1993; Clarke and Newman, 1997).

The Rise of Managerialism in the Public Sector

Whilst managerialism is not a new concept, the 1990s have seen a developing literature with managerialism and management within the public sector as its focus. Earlier, Burnham (1962), in one of the initial uses of the concept, pointed to the development of a managerial class who gain more control and influence over production and over the functions of the state. Hearn and Roberts (1976) examined managerialism in government in the 1960s and 1970s, and Flynn (1997) brought the concept into the context of the 1990s. Analysis of this development within the context of social work and welfare is evident, from Cousins (1987) and Pithouse (1989) to Clarke and Newman (1997) and Harris (1998).

The increasing emphasis on 'management' has been reinforced by the advent and consolidation of successive UK governments throughout the 1980s and 1990s. They have placed much emphasis on the effective management of resources and on a change in culture from that which the public sector and its administration had previously been seen to represent. This approach is founded on an ideology which sees the free market as being the most efficient way of allocating resources, with consumers being given more choice about the services they wish to use.

This increased choice would become available through competition and the development of markets. Further to this is the desire for a diminution of the role of the state across all activities (Metcalfe and Richards, 1987; Cutler and Waine, 1994; Flynn, 1997). A third factor influencing this development, within social welfare particularly, was dissatisfaction with welfare services, welfare organizations and welfare professionals. Professionals were seen as developing a significant power base and denying consumer choice. Their concern with issues such as equality of opportunity, anti-oppressive practice and so on were seen as trendy, irrelevant to their functions and not in the public interest. They were also seen as being in favour of increasing state involvement and thus contrary to an ideology which favoured a decreasing role for the state.

Clarke and Newman (1997) discuss a general disenchantment with the welfare state coming from various sources, and being conveniently channeled and refined by the new right in politics into a consumerist challenge to traditional organisation and its professional staff. Whilst the new right wanted to develop the power of the individual, the language of new managerialism also had an appeal to many within the welfare state - increasing control and power for managers; promoting service excellence and customer focus. Thus, it was not an imposed ideology combating direct resistance.

The climate at the time supported the arguments for free market provision of public services, when strict reductions in public sector expenditure were called for from very influential agencies notably the IMF. Pressures for change in the role of public sector management and the emphasis on management itself were partly ideological, partly pragmatic in view of financial constraints on the public purse, and partly user or consumer focused. The latter being reflected in concern with the services provided (Adams, 1998). This trend for change in public sector organisations was also felt beyond the UK (Edwards et al., 1996). Many countries encountered and continue to encounter similar pressures. These pressures have contributed to the liberalisation of their economic policies in addition to a review of their public sector organisations (Kirkpatrick and Cook, 1995).

An additional influential factor in the rise of managerialism, according to Rogers (1990), was the popularization of the literature on 'Excellence' developed by Peters and Waterman (1982). The principles this literature expounded were seen as relevant by local government and influenced what many local government managers were doing, and wanted to do, in managing their own areas of responsibility in the 1990s. This literature also provided managers with models which they could consider in the face of the new demands regarding their roles. Rogers points out that some of the messages promoted by Peters and Waterman, especially those concerning organisations being 'close to the customer', struck strong chords in many local authorities of all political complexions. They were becoming, or being made to become, more aware of what the consumers (rather than clients) wanted (rather than needed) and of the consumers' views of the services provided, rather than being concerned with ratepayers solely as funders of services. Adams (1998) also stresses the importance of this development and how it has caused managers in social work to think anew about the means to involve consumers in decision-making. Both Adams and Rogers argue that this development has generated an interest in how the commercial sector has developed such specialisms as Total Quality Management, Quality Circles and Quality Assurance and other related matters and how these can be transferred to and used in public sector organizations. Throughout the 1980s and 1990s we have seen the introduction of previously unfamiliar concepts in this context: quality management, strategy, human resource management, performance related pay, devolved management, consumer focus. These have become issues attracting a great deal of attention in both commercial and non-commercial organizations. These developments constitute a major departure from the traditional pre-occupations of senior public sector officers and demands that they employ different perspectives of their current roles and different skills from those they were accustomed to using, reinforcing the need for new perspectives and new skills in management.

Impact of Managerialism

Prior to the rise of managerialism, the purposes and processes of public sector organisations were largely decided by publicly accountable bodies and individuals. Functionaries within the organisations themselves would be responsible for ensuring that these purposes were achieved. The new approach is less about administration and more about management. It requires managers to be more active in determining policy, utilising resources effectively and evaluating outcome. This demonstrates a change of function, as administrators become managers, from one of implementing strategy imposed on them, to one where managers and management develop and implement their own strategy within a framework defined by public bodies. At service delivery levels also, managers were to be more responsible and given greater discretion, exemplifying the points made by Clarke *et al.* (1994) on the new role of management as operating at both strategic and operational levels.

The earlier impact of the rise in managerialism in local government is discussed by Elcock (1989). He points to the relative homogeneity of structure, practice and procedures in local authorities throughout a great part of this century, identifying the early 1970s as the time when local authority management first came under any real scrutiny. The traditions and values of local authority departments and the professional groups which staffed them were largely unchallenged. The changes demanded for the management of these organisations were very wide ranging. There was a succession of management developments in a number of areas, as summarised by Stewart (1989), during the initial stages of managerial changes. These developments have grown and evolved further throughout the 1990s. Such initiatives include the specification of the need: for strategic management; for devolved management responsibility in achieving strategic objectives; for review of organisational performance and the adoption of more appropriate organisational culture; and for new means of engaging staff in strategic objectives and in developing new standards of service delivery (Stewart, 1989).

The continuation of these trends to date is significant. These themes imply a change in the overall management of public sector organisations, not as a one-off institutional change but as a continuing and active process. This constitutes a change from a mechanistic, static organisation to an organic, vital organisation. This is clearly a shift away from the traditional patterns of administration which were largely unchanging and expecting not to have to change. These changes also signify a shift, in many parts of the public sector, from a 'professional' model of management - where the individual professional was relatively autonomous and where issues such as the quality of service delivery were implicit in professionalism - to a 'managerial' model which emphasises the manager's role across all the organisation's operating areas. Using the organisational models of Mintzberg (1983), the shift might be seen as one from professional bureaucracies to adhocracies to reflect the changing and increasingly unpredictable environment and the adaptive strategies of public sector organisations.

In practical terms, the effects of the change in emphasis and the concern about management can be seen in various parts of the UK public sector, such as the Civil Service, local government and the NHS, over the past number of years with the implementation of many changes. Many public sector organisations were privatised. Change was implemented across those that remained in the public sector. There was the 'Efficiency Strategy' in the Civil Service; the use of compulsory competitive tendering for contracts and now the use of 'Best Value' in local government; managerial re-structuring in health and social care; the establishment of the Audit Commission and a wider role and increasing power for the Social Services Inspectorate; the development of internal markets in health and social care; and increased emphasis on management development in public sector training organisations.

The intention to limit the scope of the public sector and to use the resources allocated to it more efficiently has resulted in an increased impetus for public sector organisations to start operating in a similar fashion to private business. The removal of the guaranteed funding of previous governments, ensured that these organisations now had to face unfamiliar problems. As public sector organisations came to share some of the problems faced by organisations in the private sphere it is not surprising that they looked to the private sector for models of how to deal with them, as will be discussed later.

Ideological developments were supported by legislative changes, for example in community care, and led to a 'managerial consciousness - the implanting of managerial frameworks of calculation, expertise and decision-making as the guiding principles of organisational action' (Charlesworth et al., 1996, p. 82). Management thus has been accepted as a set of techniques and principles, competences, skills, and functions. In many respects this has been accepted uncritically. For some writers (e.g. Hughes, 1994) the development of managerialism in this sector is seen as inevitable and as holding less threat for the public sector than its critics suggest. Other more critical views (e.g. Cutler and Wayne, 1994; Pollitt, 1993; Clarke and Newman, 1997; Harris, 1998) stress that these developments do not take place in a political vacuum. The implications of this shift and the rising importance of such issues as the performance of public/welfare organisations signify a fundamental change in the nature of welfare provision and delivery. The more critical perspectives point to the considerable divergence in how these developments might be viewed. Looking at managerialism solely as providing a set of techniques for more effective organisation is a uni-dimensional view. Largely, such writers agree in considering these developments to be a major shift in power dimensions within welfare organisations. Managerialism is viewed, not as being singly defined, but as a development which alters previous means of co-ordination and previous relationships. These now may take different forms. The prime point is that it constitutes a new order, a new framework of power:

> We are not just talking about the appointment of managers or the adoption of private sector management discourses and techniques. What is taking place, we would argue, is a deeper ideological process of managerialization which is transforming relationships of power, culture, control and accountability. In this sense, managerialization is a dynamic, transformative process which cuts across the domain of social policy, unlocking the old welfare settlement and making the quest for a definitive political reading of the new arrangements a problematic endeavour (Clarke et al., 1994, p. 3).

This argument serves to indicate the complexity of reviewing the development of managerialism in this context. There are indeed other difficulties here, not least the problematic nature of defining management itself (Hales, 1993) and of defining welfare and social work. Managers are now being asked to carry out unfamiliar roles and to use unfamiliar skills. The skills they have previously used have become either obsolete or reduced in value. Their roles and titles have changed, as has the range of tasks and the priority associated with each. Indeed there are those (e.g. Taylor, 1989) who argue that regardless of perceived identity of technician, professional or administrator, the notion that 'we are all managers now' is pervasive.

The continuing and eternal tensions and conflicts within welfare and social policy mean that we are not left and will not be left with a single definition of management or managerialism. It is one factor in a complex, dynamic debate involving professionals, policy makers, politicians and now managers. The significant development is that this debate does now involve managers as major power holders. The search for practices and principles of management to guide this development in the public sector frequently led to the private sector, despite its different aims and values, being promoted as having valuable lessons to give, if not models to adopt.

Public and Private Sectors – Influence, Difference and Convergence

From an academic perspective, writers contributing to the public-private debate use different starting points. There are those who make direct comparisons between the different sectors and identify similarities and differences (Stewart, 1989; Stewart and Ranson, 1994). There are those who use a management theory approach and look at the appropriateness and application of theory in public sector organizations (Euske and Euske, 1991). In addition there are those who use an introspective approach, considering what specific features public sector organizations may have which set them apart (Ackroyd et al., 1989). The earlier discussions on the nature of public sector organizations vis-à-vis the private sector, helped pave the way for other thinking on management in the public sector (e.g. Willcocks and Harrow, 1992; Farnham and Horton, 1993; Dunleavy and Hood, 1994; Ferlie et al., 1996; Flynn, 1997) which identifies the developing new public management ethos.

At the operational level, successive governments have actively encouraged the adoption by public sector management of private sector models (Harrow and Willcocks, 1990; Pollitt, 1993). The contribution made by eminent managers in the private sphere to the development of management practices in the public domain has illustrated how these private sector models are valued by government. Significant contributions to the change in culture and management in the NHS, in Social Services and in the Civil Service have been implemented under the guidance of senior commercial figureheads. The introduction of these models has been accompanied by the rise in concepts all relatively new to the public sector. In addition to those cited earlier, such concepts as organisational risk, entrepreneurship and consumerism are all now features of the individual, market-dominated model of public sector service and would be less familiar in the preceding collectivist and state interventionist model of public service. Whilst the concept of risk in itself is familiar in the fields of, for example, child protection and mental health, risk assessment at a strategic level was less so (Alaszewski et al., 1998). The introduction of these concepts has led to further adoption of methods from organisations who are seen as having the experience of, and expertise in, dealing with these issues.

The two popular assumptions which lie at the foundations of the debate on the application of commercial models in the public sector were well summarised by Ackroyd et al. (1989), at a time when major change in the public sector was being felt acutely. They see them as being, firstly, that public sector organizations should be managed as in the private sphere and aim to develop the same character and objectives as their private counterparts and, secondly, that public sector management is pretty much like private sector management anyway. These assumptions are recognised as being too simplistic. Ackroyd et al. reject the assumptions outlined and assert that public sector management contains very different sets of activities from the private sector, which are neither fully understood nor recognised.

In considering debates on the main differences between public and private sector organisations there is the danger of over-generalizing. There may be an assumption that homogeneity exists in each sector: that is, that all public sector organisations are very similar if not the same, and all private sector organisations are very similar. It may be an over-simplification to consider the dimension of public or private ownership as being the main distinguishing feature between organisations. Whilst certain differences are accepted, it is not the differences themselves which are the main concern, rather it is the managerial implications of those differences. Later discussions accept these differences but do not see them as a barrier preventing the implementation of new management practices. Rather, they influence the public sector to incorporate ideas from the commercial sector whilst retaining the core values of the public sector, leading to the identification and development of the 'New Public Management' (Dunleavy and Hood, 1994; Ferlie et al., 1996).

The attempt to differentiate each sector entirely, illustrates the existence of two contrasting political or ideological models, the market model and the pluralist model. This distinction implies different objectives and different processes to achieve ends, together with a more complex set of expectations in public sector organisations as noted below. The public sector also has to deal with more intangible and at times diverse objectives than their private sector counterparts. There is also a different pressure between long term and short term survival. Private sector organizations are concerned with profitability and liquidity and their higher echelons of management may feel relatively secure in their positions, provided such factors are maintained in an acceptable fashion for their shareholders. In the public sector, longer term survival of the organisation may be more assured as their existence may be demanded by statute. However, the continuation of their elected representatives may be less secure. At both national and perhaps more immediately at local government level, there is constant public pressure to replace elected representatives and to change policy. Company directors may be faced with such challenges but it is unlikely that they would be so institutionalized and public. In short therefore, accountability may be considerably heightened and more immediate in public sector organisations which face a wider range of stakeholder groups with a more varied and potentially conflicting range of interests. Interestingly, as private sector models have developed in their own ways and as the new public sector management has developed, some common elements are beginning to appear. The most notable of these is the notion of a stakeholder analysis of organisations (Hutton, 1995; Wheeler and Sillanpää, 1997; Winstanley et al., 1995; Field, 1996) or of a similar inclusive approach to management (RSA, 1995). Stakeholder interests in public sector organisations include those of people who receive services, directly and indirectly, and those who fund such services. The result of this, in combination with pressures for benchmarking, efficiency and so on, is that managers need to take account of the different ways in which these interested parties measure the performance of the operation for which the manager is responsible. It is here that both public sector and private sector may be developing similar approaches, still allowing for their respective differences.

However, the application of free market approaches to the public sector and the rise of managerialism have to be viewed with some caution. These stated ideologies of free market mechanisms and decentralization have been pursued, paradoxically, through a resort to a strong state and even an increasing centralisation of decision-making in much of the state

(Shaw, 1995). Furthermore, despite policy statements on rolling back the state and low taxation, the state continues to expand in many sectors as taxation levels continue to increase. Similar paradoxes are evident in considering repeated government attacks on quangos, alongside the subsequent expansion of such unelected bodies in and around the state. Again, paradox is apparent in the contrast between the anti-bureaucratic rhetoric of the new right and the 'new bureaucratisation' that has occurred with increased 'accountability' monitoring and evaluation, increased use of internal markets and greater regulation of and by managers in the context of institutional 'deregulation' (Harris, 1998). The comparison of public and private sector organisations also needs to acknowledge the socio-political developments which influence their respective operating domains.

There remain both significant differences between public and private sectors and areas in common. It is important to recognise both these aspects in order to establish how management within the public sector can develop.

Future Development of Public Sector Management

The influence of the commercial sector on the public sector is unlikely to diminish. However, we can see that this is not a simple process of the direct transfer of commercial management approaches across sectors, rather the development of a range of public sector management approaches. Where is this likely to lead? Ferlie *et al.* (1996) detail four models of public sector management which they see as developing in response to the pressures for change. According to their argument, there is no clear or agreed definition of the new public management. Not only this, there is continuing debate and disagreement about what it should be. They detail four models or foci of public sector management. The first is characterised by the efficiency drive, where the previous, bureaucratic structures were seen as having considerable in-built inefficiencies, which could be dealt with through private sector management methods. The second has decentralisation and downsizing as its focus, where previous structures were seen as being inadequate and the structure of the organisation should be determined more by markets as control mechanisms rather than by hierarchies. The third centres on cultural change, where the lessons from the 'Excellence' literature were implemented with the focus on values and on organisational learning. The final model has renewed public service orientation as its central value, where the distinctiveness of the public sector is recognised and where the most applicable elements of private sector methods can be adapted and implemented. A prime concern here is with the continuing legitimacy of the public sector organisation.

These models are clearly not mutually exclusive. However, they demonstrate different assumptions about the public sector and its main focus, and also highlight different emphases within the management function. Different key evaluation indicators are used depending on what the prime focus is. These models form a useful tool for analysing the development of thought and application in this context. The last model is seen as being the least developed of the four and is where current thought appears to be directed. The change in UK national government after the 1997 election also adds to the viability of this interest in a hybrid approach - public sector concern and understanding and private sector ethos and methods. The notion of a stakeholder approach to the management of public sector organisations is an indication of this. Ferlie *et al.*'s models indicate the heterogeneous nature of the public sector, different elements within the sector will themselves have different approaches and different priorities. However, the recognition that public sector management is underpinned by a particular set of values in working towards social goals, in addition to the importance of financial efficiency, is important in according this sector legitimacy. Public sector management is not a second rate set of commercial principles and practices but is management within a different context.

We can see that the concept and practices of managerialism have become increasingly important in the public sector. The influence of commercial management approaches has gained increasing acceptance, along with a growing awareness of the distinctiveness of public sector organisations. There are still, however, contested areas and particular issues which apply in the analysis of this development within social work organisations.

Managerialism and the Impact on Social Work Organisations

Whilst the previous discussion considers difference and convergence between sectors and developments in public sector management, this section focuses more directly on implications and impact within social work organisations. It is important to recognise the different locations of social work organisations both within and beyond the UK context. Within the UK the majority of social work organisations still fall within the public sector, being funded by the taxation system and being regulated as part of national or local government. Unlike some other socio-economic contexts, these organisations are separate from social security systems. There is a significant, established and growing voluntary sector which provides social work services, most notably charitable organisations. There is also a growth, concurrent with the drive for privatized services, of independent social work provision. A framework for charting the changes as they impact on public sector organsations is provided by Farnham and Horton (1993). If we consider social work organisations using this framework, we can identify changes over the recent past.

Strategic Management

Social work organisations have indeed begun to develop strategic management plans and are becoming more transparent in the establishment and progress towards achieving policy objectives (Adams, 1998). The emphasis on the strategic role of senior management is also evident in job advertisements for senior managers within social work organisations and within documents produced by such organisations, including references to 'mission statements' and 'strategic plans'.

Adaptive Structures

New organisational structures are not unusual within local government and, therefore, within local authority social services departments. There has been a trend in many local authorities to establish focal user points or 'one stop shops' where local citizens can access a variety of local services. This trend has continued under the new public management. It would be a mistake, however, to attribute this move to managerialism alone. Whilst this may have been the driving force recently for some organisations, such moves have long been part of social policy initiatives at local and national levels. These steps have been intended to encourage greater and easier access to services, indeed to 'localise' services in a way which attempts to deal with the monolithic and difficult to access bureaucratic processes which have long been said to characterise traditional local government services. There is a long established drive for user involvement in a variety of social work services (Croft and Beresford, 1990; Beresford and Croft, 1993). Thus delegation of authority and the development of more flexible services was an established trend which pre-dates the development of managerialism, though this is certainly a factor in current developments. The emphasis now on partnerships in health and social care necessitates flexibility in organisational form.

Delegated Authority

The delegation of authority to managers has undoubtedly happened in social work organisations. This has been accompanied by the establishment of managerial structures and management positions which did not exist previously (Lawler, 1993). Managers now have responsibility for budgets, teams of workers and other resources, the effective management of which is now their responsibility. There has been real delegation of managerial authority which has accompanied the specification of performance objectives. Changes in organisational structure and the allocation of identified resources to specific managers have supported this delegation. Managers have identifiable teams of workers and a strategic framework within which to locate their own operations.

Performance Measures and New Technology

There has been considerable development of measures of performance in social work organizations over recent years (Connor and Black, 1994). This has become a concern of many parties with an interest in social work services. This concern comes from: policy makers who wish to monitor policy implementation; social workers, who wish to have indicators of their own effectiveness; managers who wish to consider the broader impact of the services they manage and their value; the general public who wish to know firstly, that good quality services are being delivered and secondly, that they are so done in a cost effective manner; and users who wish to know the extent of their choice as users of services and that they are receiving appropriate and high quality services (Carter *et al.*, 1992).

Culture Change

As noted earlier, the language of business is now in regular use in the public sector, including social work organisations. Concepts such as quality management, excellence, performance appraisal are now understood and have achieved a degree of respectability in this context (Edwards *et al.*, 1996). The idea of 'learning organisations' has also been well publicized (e.g. Senge, 1992; Pedler *et al.*, 1997) but, as yet, does not appear to have been widely applied to social work organisations. The most notable development is that of private provision (competitive, albeit regulated, markets) and purchaser/provider designations (quasi-markets) together with the accompanying marketing concepts and jargon (Kelly, 1991; Wistow *et al.*, 1994; Bartlett *et al.*, 1994; Adams, 1998).

Important points are made by Bartlett *et al.* (1994) in connection with quasi-markets. They view the political dimension as key to understanding the nature of these 'markets'. They are politically constructed in that they are not competitive in the manner of commercial markets. They do not allow free entry and exit from the market, for example, social services are established by statute and cannot decide to withdraw from this market. Additionally, political intervention is possible and likely at times. This may come through direct involvement at times of crisis or change, and regularly at other times because of local and national political accountability. Despite the introduction of such markets, national and local accountability still exists through political and governmental systems. Finally and importantly, there is a political dimension for analysing the function of the organisation – this is particularly so regarding social work, that is, there are structural analyses available for considering the nature of social need and social policy initiatives which do not have direct parallels in commercial settings. Together these factors demonstrate that, whilst market principles have been introduced in social work, they have particular limitations.

Human Resource Management

Whilst there is a small but developing literature on Human Resource Management and its role in public sector organisations (e.g. Yntema, 1993; Rigg and Trehan, 1993), the change in Human Resource Management within social work organisations does not appear to have been significant (Langan and Clarke, 1994). Trades unions are still relatively strong in the areas of social work and social care and collective bargaining still characterizes much of social work employment relations. At senior levels, however, more individualized contracts are in evidence (Farnham and Horton, 1993). The scale of the introduction of such systems as performance appraisal for social work practitioners is at this stage unknown and further research is needed to address this. The particular issue of the management of professional staff within social work is discussed later.

Public Service Orientation

Social work organisations are clearly being influenced to consider demand-led rather than supply led services and to consider those who use social work services as 'users' or even 'consumers' rather than the 'clients' of old (Butcher, 1995). This is, however, an area riven with potential problems, not least of which is that of limited choice, lack of purchasing power as in a commercial exchange, and the lack of power in relation to professional workers. In addition, there may be little discretion as to whether to use the service or not, i.e. some service users of child care or mental health services, may not be using the service through their own choice (Adams, 1998). They are 'reluctant users' of such services and the consumerist model of choice in the market is clearly inadequate here. In a free market the consumer is in a powerful position. In terms of social work, ill-informed and vulnerable service users may not be in the best position to estimate the quality of care they receive. Shaw (1995) argues that fundamentally consumerism in this context is flawed. Consumers are not sovereign: they are in need, they are vulnerable. They do not necessarily themselves demand services but are represented by agents and as such do not have commercial consumer power; they may not use services voluntarily; their choice may be very limited by the localised availability of services and by local, informal, rationing processes. Whilst aspects of consumerism may be found in social work organisations, the public service ethos remains significant in the design and delivery of services.

From the above points it can be seen that the impact of managerialism within the context of UK social work, is considerable indeed. This must not, however, be seen as a complete transition from one status to another. The specific literature on management within social work (Coulshed, 1990; Bamford, 1982) and on the organisations which manage and deliver social work services (Challis, 1990) is by no means extensive. Even less is written from the perspective of social work managers themselves (Lawler and Hearn, 1997). Certain literature on management in social work takes a labour process view rather than a management perspective (for example, see Harris, 1998). The indications are that whilst managerialism is impacting significantly on social work organisations, this is not supported by the recruitment of managers from outside social work with different work experience. It would appear that the vast majority of social work managers still have backgrounds either in social work or in some closely related profession such as nursing (Lawler, 1993), though there are indications of some developments here (Dominelli and Hoogvelt, 1996).

Whilst this framework is useful in assessing the impact of managerialism in social work, it does not take sufficient account of the issues involved in the management of a professional body of staff, which will be considered next.

Management of Professional Staff

A significant characteristic of social work organisations is the body of professional social work staff employed. In an era of increased managerial responsibility, how are such staff to be 'managed'? In addition to the general management issues facing social work managers this poses a particular challenge. Professional social workers form a significant group of workers in social work organisations not only numerically but also in terms of the scope of their decision-making. Such professional groups may indeed resist the development of the managerial ethos as being a kerb on the traditional role of professionals. Such professionals are used to exercising autonomy of decision-making both in the assessment of need and in the allocation of resources. Their training, knowledge and experience enable them to make decisions in relation to service users, whose needs are often complex. The extent of this autonomy is changing due to greater management control. One consequence is increased tension between professionals and managers.

This is not the only development affecting the professional role in social work. There is a separate trend to de-professionalise certain elements of the service, enabling unqualified staff to carry out certain tasks under professional supervision, thus reducing the need to employ professionals (Cannen, 1994/5). Professionals may, therefore, see themselves as being under threat in two respects: their work being under great managerial control on the one hand and being under threat of de-professionalisation or fragmentation on the other. Additionally, there is the general suspicion with which professional groups have been viewed by successive governments. The resulting defensiveness of professionals may complicate the manager's job all the more (Edwards et al., 1996). Traditionally, professional social workers were supervised by senior professional workers. This was seen as an appropriate relationship. Professional supervision has now been augmented by management supervision. Social workers' practice is now under direct scrutiny from managers. This relationship may be more problematic and signifies a distinct change from the 'invisibility' of the social work process (Pithouse, 1989) which previously characterised it. Accountability then was internal, part of supervisory relationship and a facet of professional autonomy. It is now becoming more overt, external and managerial. Decisions previously made by social workers, particularly concerning the allocations of resources, are now made by managers. This shift in the locus of control for decision-making is noted by Charlesworth *et al.* (1996). Recent developments have therefore seen a shift from a bureau-professional means of co-ordination and operation to a managerial means. Key decisions, criteria for making those decisions and the resources to support decisions now rest with managers. They now have considerably more influence over these than professionals and administrators had in the preceding regime.

Pressure for greater transparency of the social work process and accountability for its outcomes may be seen as desirable in pursuing public goals and in monitoring the performance of publicly employed professionals, but there may be less positive consequences also. Adams argues that in the worst scenarios managerialism 'constrains professional autonomy and limits or undermines its effectiveness' (Adams, 1998, p. 39). He argues that it may be the service itself and its recipients who are affected ultimately by the reduction in autonomy. The increase in written procedures and the development of competences in social care leave less room for discretion, less understanding of the depth of some of the issues involved in the delivery of the service, and less autonomy in decision making. The result may be an inability to challenge some of the oppressive practices carried out by and within social work organisations (Dominelli, 1996). The aspect of changing power relationships is discussed by Shaw (1995), who outlines the critiques of professional power which were topical in the 1970s and the reaction to the potential oppression of professional power, particularly in social care and health care. These debates have come back to haunt professionals, who previously may have subscribed themselves to these views. This argument was used by successive conservative governments as justification for the reduction in social workers' power and an increase in managerial power.

Is it possible then that the continuing role of the professional social work is under threat? If so, what is the likely resolution of these dilemmas? There are arguments that some accommodation may be possible. Occupants of managerial roles may identify themselves both as managerial and professional (Lawler, 1993) but there are tensions between the identities. Professional co-ordination has not been substituted by managerialism but a more complex dynamic now exists between the two. In some cases professional-managerial hybrids now exist (Charlesworth et al., 1996). Clarke and Newman (1997) also point to 'hybrid' managers/professionals as developing in some areas. They also argue that managers have not supplanted professionals but that professional work has been subordinated to management. The development of hybrid managers may grow as management incorporates concepts such as standards of service and quality of delivery in addition to their concern with efficiency. In other respects it can be argued that this accommodation is unlikely because the skills and expertise needed for each role are not complementary. Tensions within such roles are likely to continue.

In some respects a change of roles has resulted, for example, the introduction of a care manager role with a high emphasis on managerial rather than professional skills. This constitutes a significant departure from the preceding culture and systems (Langan and Clarke, 1994). Social work becomes the service which is purchased and care management is the co-ordination and commissioning of that service. Social worker and care manager may be partners but they are distinct with different skills and different priorities. Professionals may find themselves in a difficult position. If they accept totally the new managerial status quo they may be seen in a poor light by their peers. If they resist such developments they may be seen as obstructive. In their attempts to maintain professional autonomy and in their eyes to protect standards of service delivery, they may be accused of undermining the service (Cutler and Waine, 1994). They risk being 'perceived as dissidents working to undermine quality assurance, rather than acting as its guardians, by critically scrutinizing the assumptions on which prevalent methods are based' (Adams, 1998, p. 61).

Jones (1999) implies that professionals in social work have become increasingly marginalised, partly as a result of managerialism but partly because of their own inability to resist becoming agents of the state. They have accepted social policy changes passively and, as a result, are now acting against rather than on behalf of their clients' interests. The introduction of management philosophies, the reduction of professional autonomy and the diminution of professional input into the social work training agenda have all conspired to reduce the power of the professional, both at individual and collective levels.

Whilst there is evident concern with effectiveness and efficiency in social work organisations, as noted above, significantly less is made of the management of people. In this setting, there are particular issues relating to the management of people, for example, the changed 'psychological contract', which follows a change in employment conditions. Additionally professional, self-managed staff have lost significant autonomy and need their professional skills to be 'managed' in a way which is quite different from before. This in itself, constitutes a significant departure and is not well addressed in the literature. Perhaps there is an assumption that in such a context where 'caring' for people is central to the function of the organisation, social workers promoted to management levels already have sufficient 'people skills' to render any discussion of how these skills might be developed as irrelevant. It is interesting that this issue receives such little attention, in a context where relationships with people form such a core focus of work.

Concluding Comments

Several challenges exist for social work organisations facing this period of managerial transition. These are discussed in detail elsewhere (Lawler and Hearn, 1997) but merit note here. For example, if most managers have been professional social workers, career development opportunities for social workers is an important issue. More management development opportunity is needed for those who elect a management career and whose background and training do not necessarily equip them with the requisite skills and concepts for management roles. Furthermore, the training of social workers may need to be amended to incorporate wider aspects of management in the curriculum if they are to become care managers or resource managers relatively early in their professional careers. Alternatively, if senior professionals have no formal exposure to management and management training, senior levels of management will ultimately be populated by managers without social work backgrounds, recruited externally (Charlesworth *et al.*, 1996). Finally, social policy development needs to review the operation of the newly constituted organsational arrangements and also to review the performance of managers within this context. There are several dimensions to assessing the effectiveness of managers here. Evaluation is needed of: effectively managing the organisation itself, serving users and meeting their needs; and pursuing and achieving social policy objectives. If some balance between professional and managerial concerns is not achieved, the implications are that professional work and values will be subsumed beneath a focus exclusively on efficiency and effectiveness.

We do not know and cannot predict the likely forms and impact of managerialism in the next decade but developments in social work organisations will be strongly influenced by responses to these challenges.

References

Ackroyd, S., Hughes, J.A. and Soothill, K. (1989), 'Public Services and their Management', *Journal of Management Studies*, vol. 26, no. 6, pp. 602-19.
Adams, R. (1998), *Quality Social Work*, Macmillan, Basingstoke.
Alaszewski, A., Harrison, L. and Manthorpe, J. (eds) (1998), *Risk, Health and Welfare*, Open University Press, Buckingham.
Bamford, T. (1982), *Managing Social Work*, Tavistock, London.
Bartlett, W., Propper, C., Wilson, D. and Le Grande, J. (1994), *Quasi-Markets in the Welfare State*, SAUS, Bristol.
Beresford, P. and Croft, S. (1993), *Citizen Involvement: a practical guide for change*, Macmillan/BASW, London.
Burnham, J. (1962), *The Managerial Revolution*, Penguin, Harmondsworth.
Butcher, T. (1995), *Delivering Welfare Services*, Open University Press, Buckingham.
Cannen, C. (1994/5), 'Enterprise Culture, Professional Socialisation and Social Work Education in Britain', *Critical Social Policy*, vol. 42, Winter pp. 5-19.
Carter, N., Klein, R. and Day, P. (1992), *How Organisations Measure Success*, Routledge, London.
Challis, L. (1990), *Organising Public Social Services*, Longman, Harlow.
Charlesworth, J., Clarke, J. and Cochrane, A. (1996), 'Tangled Webs? Managing Local Mixed Economies of Care', *Public Administration*, vol. 47, Spring, pp. 67-88.
Clarke, J., Cochrane, A. and McLaughlin, E. (eds) (1994), *Managing Social Policy*, Sage, London.
Clarke, J. and Newman, J. (1997), *The Managerial State*, Sage, London.
Connor, A. and Black, S. (eds) (1994), *Performance Review and Quality in Social Care*, Research Highlights in Social Work 20, Jessica Kingsley, London and Bristol.
Coulshed, V. (1990), *Management in Social Work*, Macmillan, Basingstoke.
Cousins, C. (1987), *Controlling Social Welfare: a Sociology of State Welfare Work and Organisation*, Wheatsheaf, Brighton.
Croft, S. and Beresford, P. (1990), *From Paternalism to Participation: Involving People in Services*, London, Open Services Project/Joseph Rowntree.
Cutler, T. and Waine, B. (1994), *Managing the Welfare State*, Berg, Oxford.
Dixon, J., Kouzmin, A. and Korac-Kakabadse, N. (1998), 'Managerialism – Something Old, Something Borrowed, Little New. Economic Prescription versus Effective Organisational Change in Public Agencies', *International Journal of Public Sector Management*, vol. 11, no. 2/3, pp. 164-87.
Dominelli, L. (1996), 'Deprofessionalising Social Work: Equal Opportunities, Competences and Post-Modernism', *British Journal of Social Work*, vol. 26, pp. 153-75.

Dominelli, L. and Hoogvelt, A. (1996), 'Globalization and the Technocratization of Social Work', *Critical Social Policy*, vol. 16, no. 4, pp. 45-62.
Dunleavy, P. and Hood, C. (1994), 'From Old Administration to New Public Management', *Public Money and Management*, vol. 14, no. 3, pp. 9-16.
Edwards, R.L., Cooke, P.W. and Nelson Reid, P. (1996), 'Social Work Management in an Era of Diminished Federal Responsibility', *Social Work*, vol. 41, pp. 468-79.
Elcock, H. (1989), 'The Changing Management of Local Government' in I. Taylor and G. Popham (eds), *An Introduction to Public Sector Management*, Unwin Hyman, London.
Euske, N.A. and Euske, K.J. (1991), 'Institutional Theory: Employing the Other Side of Rationality in Non-Profit Organizations', *British Journal of Management*, vol. 2, pp. 81-8.
Farnham, D. and Horton, S. (eds) (1993), *Managing the New Public Services*, Macmillan, Basingstoke.
Ferlie, E., Ashburner, L., Fitzgerald, L. and Pettigrew, A. (1996), *The New Public Management in Action*, Oxford University Press, Oxford.
Field, F. (1996), *Stakeholder Welfare*, IEA, London.
Flynn, N. (1990), *Public Sector Management*, Harvester Wheatsheaf, Hemel Heampstead.
Flynn, N. (1997), *Public Sector Management* (third edition), Prentice Hall Harvester Wheatsheaf, London.
Hales, C. (1993), *Managing Through Organisation: the Management Process, Form of Organisation and the Work of Managers*, Routledge, London.
Harris, J. (1998), *Managing State Social Work: Front Line Management and the Labour Process Perspective*, Ashgate, Aldershot.
Harrow, J. and Willcocks, L. (1990), 'Public Services Management: Activities, Initiatives and Limits to Learning', *Journal of Management Studies*, vol. 27, no. 3, pp. 281-303.
Hearn, J. and Roberts, I. (1976), 'Planning Under Difficulties: The Move to Decrementalism' in K. Jones, (ed.), *The Yearbook of Social Policy In Britain*, Routledge and Kegan Paul, London.
Hughes, O.E. (1994), *Public Management and Administration: An Introduction*, Macmillan, Basingstoke.
Hutton, W. (1995), *The State We're In*, Jonathan Cape, London.
Jones, C. (1999), 'Social Work: Regulation and Managerialism', in M. Exworthy and S. Halford (eds), *Professionals and the New Managerialism in the Public Sector*, Open University Press, Buckingham.
Keen, L. and Scase, R. (1996), 'Middle Managers and the New Managerialism', *Local Government Studies*, vol. 22, no. 4, pp. 167-86.
Kelly, A. (1991), 'The 'New' Managerialism in the Social Services' in P. Carter, T. Jeffs, and M. Smith (eds), *Social Work and Social Welfare Yearbook 3*, Open University Press, Milton Keynes.
Kirkpatrick, C. and Cook, P. (1995), 'Privatisation Policy and Performance' in C. Kirkpatrick and P. Cook, *Privatisation Policy and Performance: International Perspectives*, Prentice Hall Harvester Wheatsheaf, Hemel Hempstead.
Langan, M. and Clarke, J. (1994), 'Managing in the Mixed Economy of Care' in J. Clarke, A. Cochrane and E. McLaughlin (eds), *Managing Social Policy*, Sage, London.
Lawler, J. (1993), 'The Social Services Manager', Unpublished PhD Thesis, Univeristy of Bradford.

Lawler, J. and Hearn, J. (1997), The Managers of Social Work: the Experiences and Identifications of Third Tier Social Services Managers and the Implications for Future Practice, *British Journal of Social Work*, vol. 27, pp. 191-218.

Metcalfe, L. and Richards, S. (1987), *Improving Public Management*, Sage, London.

Mintzberg, H. (1983), *Structure in Fives: Designing Effective Organisations*, Prentice Hall, Englewood Cliffs.

Pedler, M., Burgoyne, J. and Boydell, T. (1997), *The Learning Company: A Strategy for Sustainable Development*, (second edition), McGraw Hill, Maidenhead.

Peters, T. and Waterman, R.H. (1982), *In Search of Excellence*, Harper and Rowe, London.

Pithouse, A. (1989), *Social Work: The Organisation of an Invisible Trade*, Avebury, Aldershot.

Pollitt, C. (1993), *Managerialism and the Public Services*, (second edition), Blackwell, Oxford.

Rigg, C. and Trehan, K. (1993), 'The Changing Management of Human Resources in Local Government', in K. Isaac-Henry, C. Painter and C. Barnes (eds), *Management in the Public Sector*, Chapman and Hall, London.

Rogers, S. (1990), *Performance Management in Local Government*, Longman, Harlow.

RSA Inquiry (1995), *Tomorrow's Company*, Gower, London.

Senge, P.M. (1992), *The Fifth Discipline: the Art and Practice of the Learning Organisation*, Century Business, London.

Shaw, I. (1995), 'The Quality of Mercy. The Management of Quality in the Personal Social Services', in I. Kirkpatrick and M. Martinez Lucio (eds), *The Politics of Quality in the Public Sector*, Routledge, London.

Stewart, J. (1989), 'Management in the Public Domain', *Local Government Studies*, vol. 15, no. 5, pp. 9-16.

Stewart, J. and Ranson, S. (1994), *Management for the Public Domain: Enabling the Learning Society*, Macmillan, London.

Taylor, I. (1989), 'Introduction: Issues and Trends in Public Sector Management', in I. Taylor and G. Popham (eds), *An Introduction to Public Sector Management*, Unwin Hyman, London.

Wheeler, D. and Sillanpää, M. (1997), *The Stakeholder Corporation: a Blueprint for Maximising Stakeholder Value*, Pitman, London.

Willcocks, L. and Harrow, J. (1992), *Rediscovering Public Sector Management*, McGraw Hill, Maidenhead.

Winstanley, D., Sorabji, D. and Dawson, S. (1995), 'When the Pieces Don't Fit: A Stakeholder Power Matrix to Analyse Public Sector Restructuring', *Public Money and Management*, April-June, pp. 9-26.

Wistow, G., Knapp, M., Hardy, B. and Allen, C. (1994), *Social Care in a Mixed Economy*, Open University Press, Buckingham.

Yntema, P. (1993), 'Managing Human Resources in the Public Sector', in J. Kooiman and K.A. Eliassen (eds), *Managing Public Organisations*, Sage, London.

3 Developments in Services for Elderly People: Managing the Changes

KIT HALL AND CAROL JONES

Introduction

The history of care services for older people since the creation of generic Social Services Departments (SSDs) in the early 1970s provides a fascinating study of the development of social policy and practice. The organisation of services for this section of the public demonstrates the changing combination of service providers. All sectors are involved - informal, public, commercial and voluntary. The combination continues to change in terms of the proportion and nature of the care offered. Changes concerning the provision of care are closely connected to the increased recognition of older people's rights to have their needs met (Doyal, 1993) as well as the right to exercise choice (as consumers) in the services they receive (Butcher, 1995). Additionally, there have been significant demographic developments, and the demands of caring for an increasing number of older people have been highlighted. Themes in this debate echo those in other areas of social care. Should care be institution or community based? Who should fund care wherever it is provided? What degree of choice should be available? These enduring themes, acknowledged in chapter 1, occur again here.

Since the establishment of SSDs in the 1970s, three distinct phases in the provision of services for older people can be identified. In the early years, SSDs dominated residential and home care services. In the late 1980s and early 1990s the development of the principle of a market based community care policy influenced residential and then home care services. Since 1997, the Labour government has introduced its own vision of welfare provision. A vast array of policy initiatives have been introduced (Day, 1999; George, 1999). The White Paper on the modernisation of social services (DofH, 1998) is one initiative that will have a crucial impact on shaping the future organization and delivery of services. This document outlines the need for a 'third way' for social care. In contrast to the Conservatives, the Labour government takes an agnostic stance on the merits of state or private services. Instead of emphasising private provision, attention is directed to the quality of services experienced by individuals and families. It is the purpose of this chapter to illustrate these developments by focusing on the provision of services to older people in one particular SSD: in this regard, the chapter is a case study which illustrates not only the successes, but also the tensions and difficulties in changing policies and practice.

The authority in question covers a population of 800,000. There is a mixture of urban areas with pockets of social deprivation, more affluent conurbation and large rural areas. Since the early 1980s, the authority has been under the political control of the Labour group. Over the last two decades the structure of this particular authority has turned full circle. There has been a move away from centralised to decentralised services and now the shift is back towards centralisation, although purportedly with a more flexible structure. From the mid-1970s to 1992, the SSD was organised into 13 area offices each having responsibility for fieldwork and domiciliary services. The management of residential and day care was centralised. These areas were then reorganised into nine districts which were given responsibility for fieldwork, residential and day care services within their geographic boundaries. Following the local government reorganisation in April 1998, two districts were transferred to the new unitary city council, and the county authority in question now has seven districts. Each of these seven districts is coterminous with seven newly created Primary Care Groups. It is hoped that this (very brief) history of reorganisation gives some indication of the level of structural change that has been experienced over recent years but also the organisational context for the following discussion on service provision.

The 1970s to the 1990s: From Service Led to Needs Led Provision

In the 1970s the provision of social work and social care in the department followed a fairly common national pattern (Challis, 1990). Social work support to older people was largely provided via generic social work teams. Throughout the 1970s and 1980s the local authority was a significant provider of residential care homes for older people. This was a centralised, bureaucratic regime which delivered a resource-led service: that is, decisions about what services were to be provided were made largely on the basis of the availability of current services. The system allowed little attention to differing individual circumstances. The referral and accompanying documentation assumed that residential care would be the outcome for the older person. Alternative services were largely absent and the choice of facility was very limited, particularly in rural areas. Inevitably this resulted in some waiting lists for admission to residential homes.

At this time, most of the work with older people in the department was undertaken by unqualified workers. There was indeed, little need for professional social work discretion because of the way the services were structured. These unqualified workers were part of a traditional bureaucratic local authority management structure. Many senior social workers were under pressure to prioritise the incoming child care work, and although qualified social workers carried generic caseloads, the proportion of their client-focused work directed towards older people was often minimal. A significant proportion of referrals relating to older people were direct requests for services, for example, for home care support, residential or day care. There was no expectation of an overall assessment of need nor indeed the departmental systems to ensure that other needs were considered. The main task was to match users to requested services.

Residential service user choice was initially limited by the comparatively small role in residential care taken by the independent sector. This situation changed rapidly from the mid-1980s as the private sector saw the commercial opportunities of providing services in this area and entered the newly constituted market for care services. This expansion was not accompanied by the requirement for an assessment of need. The benefit system at the time supported anyone entering a private care home, providing their savings were below a particular capital limit. No assessment of care needs was made by either the local authority or the Department of Social Security (DSS). Although many social workers did try initially to establish that admission to care was the most appropriate option for the client, once it became apparent that this was the likely outcome and that the person would qualify for supplementary benefit, they and/or their families would be provided with a list of registered homes (if they wished to pursue placement in the independent sector) and advised to liaise with the DSS regarding funding. The 1980s saw the predicted increase in the numbers of older people, particularly the more vulnerable group of those over 80 years old. Unsurprisingly, by the end of the 1980s public expenditure on people in private care via the supplementary benefit system had rocketed.

In addition to residential facilities, the SSD traditionally operated a home care support service for a range of users. However, this service was used predominantly by older people. Domiciliary services staff were located in each geographical area. These in turn managed local teams of home helps. A referral request resulted in a visit to the potential service user by a member of the domiciliary services staff. This process was again largely administrative. Indeed, many home care managers moved into these posts from administrative assistants roles without social qualifications or experience. Different skills, such as numeracy, were seen as core to the job. Whilst this was not an established professional social work service, it did allow the development of a group of workers who gained expertise in understanding the needs of older people. In addition, these workers gained a good knowledge base of local resources. Indeed, in some instances it was the domiciliary officers who identified gaps in service provision for older people in their areas and who were at the forefront of encouraging new developments and improvements in service. However, professional social work expertise was lacking.

In the late 1980s, as generic teams could not meet the increasing demands placed on them for child care services, a national trend towards specialisms began to develop. This trend was encouraged with the introduction of the NHS and Community Care Act (1990). Following this legislation, the local authority introduced new assessment and care management teams. The ethos of this development emphasised the role of choice for the service user: that is, a choice of options of the same service (between different residential homes, for example) and choice of whether to enter a residential establishment or stay at home by means of supporting services. The additional services required to facilitate this level of choice would not automatically be provided by the local authority, but by the full range of potential service providers. As indicated above, this shift in policy was both an attempt to treat elderly people with greater respect but also to reduce the escalating costs of residential accommodation. A full assessment of need was the way in which the optimum package of care could be arrived at. Once need had been determined, relevant services could be purchased from the most appropriate provider. In consequence, the separation of the purchaser, or 'commissioners', from providers of services, enforced organisational change on an authority whose own elected controlling group held quite different political views on the mixed economy of care.

The implementation of the NHS and Community Care Act (1990) had two main thrusts which affected the way services were to be provided. The first was the transfer of financial responsibility for the purchase of residential and nursing care from the DSS to local authority SSDs. This budget became finite, thus reflecting the government's wish to bring escalating costs under control. The new financial responsibilities brought a wider range of people within the SSD net. However, users would now need an assessment of their finances to determine the extent to which they were seen as self-supporting. The second development made essential the professional assessment of need. Together these changes dictated a more sophisticated and comprehensive reflection on the needs of each individual. On the basis of the assessment, services would be commissioned. Although services were not well developed at this stage there was a slow transformation taking shape. The move was away from a bureaucratic, resource-led approach, to one increasingly based on both professional definitions of need and consumer choice.

As a means of implementing change, the department designed a suitable configuration of services in which a number of district offices were identified as pilot areas for home care assessment teams. The fundamental premise of the arrangement was that requests for home care would be directed to assessment workers whose role would be to assess the need for home care. In practice, this transitional period demonstrated a contradiction of the philosophy of needs-led assessment and a continuation of resource-led services under another guise. Whilst the role of individual assessment was recognised, services were still delivered largely on the basis of the availability of existing services, not on whether they directly addressed the needs of users. Further development of services would be necessary before a wide range of individual needs could be addressed. Gradually, the number of independent sector home care providers increased, providing the opportunity for more flexible and imaginative packages of care to be introduced, and more people to be supported in their own homes. However, the skills required to manage and co-ordinate services in this new mixed economy were lacking.

This new approach required social workers to use significant financial skills in assessing users' monetary circumstances. Under the new community care arrangements in which quasi-markets in social care were established, home care managers became service providers and social workers became commissioners or purchasers of those services. Thus, new skills were required but there was an absence of training or preparation. The authority continued to be a strong supporter of its own services, to the extent that any request for home care service was automatically directed to in-house provision. In time, permission was given for independent sector agencies to be approached when there was assessed need which the SSD could not meet. Gradually the concepts of user choice and flexibility became more evident in practice. However, the responsibility for purchasing home care services differed across districts. This led to inconsistencies and confusion over respective roles in the process. Whilst the ethos behind the changes was of competition and separation of purchasing from provision, in reality the picture was less clear than this.

In the new, competitive, market context, residential care has posed the biggest challenge to the authority in terms of whether it should or could remain a direct provider or whether it should adopt an exclusively purchaser role. Locally, there has been continuing strong political commitment to providing services, in spite of the central government agenda at that time, which saw privatisation as a central policy plank. Belief was that standards of care in the homes were generally good, although by the late 1990s the local authority found that approximately half its residential stock was significantly below the levels required by guiding standards both in terms of staffing levels and physical conditions. This had resulted from annual budget cuts which reduced money for refurbishment. The authority's homes for elderly people were frequently attractive old houses where adaptation work was prohibitively expensive. Staffing costs and overall unit costs were high because of the existing managerial structures and conditions of service.

The policy of community care was informed by the desire to increase user choice and empowerment and to co-ordinate services on the basis of need (see Griffiths, 1988). Additionally, expenditure reduction in the face of increasing demand was a prime factor. Whilst increased user choice was apparent after these changes, reduced expenditure was not. At times, independent sector providers were only used for the work that the SSD found hard to provide for itself: for example, services in remote country areas, or for covering at busy times when authority staff resources were insufficient to deal with demand. Effective models of contracting developed slowly in some areas, with the result that independent provision was commissioned via expensive spot contracts. This not only resulted in pressure on SSD budgets it also failed to provide an environment conducive to stabilising the independent sector. Uncertainty about future work demands led to a reluctance in the independent sector to develop a stable staff group. There was consequent difficulty in meeting service requests and in extreme circumstances some independent providers withdrew provision.

New policies concerning community care sought commitment to its principles, and to the assessment process itself, from colleagues in health and housing. Senior managers have worked closely with health authorities and trusts and there has been a strong commitment to joint working. At times this has been a challenging process because changed practice in one organisation impacted upon the workload of the other. Closure of long stay hospital beds and discharge procedures have contributed to the demands placed upon the SSD. The internal organisation of health services along purchaser/provider lines with health authorities, trusts and GPs has added to the complexity and problem of achieving consistency of practice. If an older person or their family is told by a medical practitioner, whether from primary care or in a hospital setting, that they need institutional care, it usually proves extremely difficult to persuade them to consider an alternative community based solution.

In summary, by the mid-1990s social work for older people was increasingly provided on a specialist basis by managers and staff committed to high professional standards. They were alert to issues of older people having choices and being given support to remain in their own homes. These teams were seeking to practice in a manner according with community care principles and welcomed the attention given to the needs of their client group. Their role, however, frequently put them in conflict with other agencies and families who were used to receiving what they had requested without too close an examination of whether support could be provided in another way. Despite this new emerging professionalism, standards and practices across the authority were variable and social work with older people was still a demand-led service in many respects.

1997 Onwards: New Government, New Approaches

Since its election in 1997 the new Labour government has demonstrated a strong commitment to the reform and modernisation of health and social services. The principles underpinning the government's strategy are evident in the White Paper 'Modernising Social Services' (DofH, 1998). In general, the government aims to increase the protection offered to vulnerable children and adults. There should be an improvement in the co-ordination of services. With this in mind, SSDs and health authorities should work in partnership. This should overcome the tensions and difficulties that previously occurred over the provision of services to elderly people and 'bed-blocking'. Services provided should be more flexible and there should be a greater clarity concerning the role of SSDs and the standards of service that might be expected. Furthermore, there should be a consistency of service and authorities should continue to improve efficiency. For services to elderly people in particular, principles concerning the promotion of independence apply. In addition, there will be a greater effort to ensure that there is fair access to services and that these services will comply with a minimum standard. Finally, a Long-term Care Charter is promised. This will attempt to ensure that services are tailored to individual needs. Satisfaction surveys will be carried out as a means of providing SSDs with information on their performance.

As noted above, in contrast with its outgoing predecessor, the government is agnostic about who provides the service. Instead, the focus is on the quality of the service and the satisfaction of the user. This principle is evident in the government's initiative concerning 'Best Value'. This was a successor to the previous imperative of compulsory competitive tendering in the delivery of services. The latter enforced a more open market in the provision of services previously run exclusively by local authorities. The 'Best Value' philosophy attempts to combine economic efficiency with a high quality of service, as opposed to an exclusive focus on cost. 'Best Value' requires authorities to measure and demonstrate quality standards (see Cirell and Bennett, 1999). Establishing transparent standards and identifying improvement has not traditionally been a strength of local government. However, it has received increasing attention in recent years (see for example, Beazley, 1994; DofH, 1992; Kelly and Warr, 1992) and has been increasingly embraced in practice within the department.

In response to these new developments the department conducted an overall review of services to elderly people. Reported here are the key findings in relation to home and residential care. With regards to home care, it was found that the in-house service is valued by users for its quality and reliability. However, it was apparent that there was a significant differential in cost between the services provided by SSD and independent providers. Furthermore, this differential could not be justified by standards of quality alone. This cost variation resulted from: different terms and conditions of service for staff; management overheads; and relatively high levels of staff absence within the authority. As a result of these conclusions, the authority has proposed to: change the organisational structure of the service; change the in-house conditions of service; improve the methods of evaluating the quality of performance; and change the contracting arrangements with the independent sector. However, these proposals are still subject to further consideration.

The review also encouraged the comparison of home care service management with other local authorities. Some authorities have developed a model of trading or business unit management. The main advantage of this approach is the ability of such a unit to operate in an entrepreneurial style, mirroring the independent organisations with whom it is competing. This allows it to become more flexible, and makes its management and operating costs more transparent. There is also the potential for income generation. Such a unit in the department could facilitate the consistency of performance. It could also build up specialist knowledge of the field which may enable a more rapid response to legislation, policy directives and service user requirements. However, these practices might also be achieved through other centrally managed models. Further implications of this approach are discussed below.

As noted above, the department's review took into account residential services to elderly people. As a consequence, there has been a recommendation that the authority should reduce its own residential provision by approximately 50 per cent over the next five years. However, as well as closing and selling off old homes, it will invest in five new homes. The process of consultation demonstrated overwhelming support for the authority to retain the direct management of the service, but it also showed that some buildings needed to be replaced because of low physical standards and high running costs. The objective is for staffing levels and buildings to meet the governments guiding standards and to meet principles of 'Best Value' in terms of quality and cost. Each new home will have 60 beds, in four distinctive living areas. Physical standards will be high: for example, *en-suite* facilities will be available. In order to provide a continuity of care from day care through respite care to full-time care, each home with have a 20 place day centre. In accordance with the expressed policy of greater partnership arrangements, there is also scope to explore the provision of health services within the establishments. The design will enable homes to be flexible in meeting specialist needs, such as older people with mental health problems, learning disabilities, physical and sensory impairment, and also to address the needs of ethnic minorities. There is additional scope for joint health and social care schemes of assessment and rehabilitation: for example, transitional bed schemes aimed at people not quite well or confident enough to return home from hospital, or where further time is required to arrange care at home, or for people experiencing temporary difficulty at home. The department's review has also identified specific targets for services for older people. Targets involve an increase in the number of service hours offered, providing guaranteed standards for continuity of service, increasing numbers of staff on NVQ programmes, user surveys to obtain qualitative feedback and better computer technologies which will improve the collection and use of management information.

Since the Labour government came into power the department has felt more secure in its position as a provider as well as co-ordinator of care. It now has to demonstrate its ability to do this by meeting a set of standards. The department sees this as a more 'objective' position to that taken by the Conservative government which saw local authority provision as philosophically unacceptable. As a result, service provision by SSDs was hedged by unfair conditions. In keeping with this, there is some indication that the Labour government is sympathetic to removing the residential allowance in the private sector which has served to make local authority homes less competitive. Despite this greater sense of security, the department, in common with all SSDs, remains in a state of flux. Given the number of policy developments initiated since 1997 this is not surprising. In its attempts to respond to the principles set out in the White Paper on modernisation of the social services (DofH, 1998), the department is making changes in relation to: partnerships with other welfare agencies; the structure of the department; and staff development. Whilst these initiatives have been acknowledged to some extent in the preceding discussion, they will each be further detailed below.

Partnerships with Other Welfare Agencies

Partnerships with other health and social care agencies are increasingly important. Both government policy and the department's review of residential facilities have helped re-focus departmental energy on relationships with housing departments and housing associations. Such organisations can contribute to the maintenance of people in the community. Consequently, a number of schemes are either in train or under exploration which will provide high levels of home care support to people living in sheltered accommodation. The need for medical support has also brought health into this arena. Hence, there is potential for constructive multi-agency partnerships and innovative practice developments. The need to develop inter-agency working in order to build a comprehensive view of users' needs requires additional communication and enhanced skills in negotiation.

Relationships with independent providers are also crucial. The department's strategic objective is to reduce care in institutional settings and increase the provision of support for needs which result from earlier hospital discharge. In order to achieve this, home care services will have to be restored to 1993 levels. On top of this, there will be an increase to reflect the estimated growth in the county population of people aged over 75. It is intended that there will be change in the overall 'mix' of care providers. At present, the department provides 80 per cent of these support services whilst the independent sector provides 20 per cent. It is anticipated that the balance of responsibility for direct service provision will change to 60/40 (approximately) by April 2001. To some extent this reflects the fact that, due to low unit costs, independent providers are often more able to offer support services more cheaply than the local authority. Partnership arrangements with the independent sector become crucial in ensuring that services are complementary. For example, the authority's home care service operates over a seven day week and has some flexibility. However, differing contractual arrangements over hours and time of work together with local 'custom and practice', reduces the availability of SSD staff. The lower costs in the independent sector have resulted in a reliance upon external providers for cover during unsociable hours. This is a situation that has developed incrementally but, in future, such arrangements need to be negotiated as part of an overall strategy to ensure a regular and consistent service.

In summary, the changes initiated by the NHS and Community Care Act (1990) and reinforced by further policy directives, will continue into the next millennium. They all require the development of a flexible range of quality services with a continuing emphasis on helping people to live independently for as long as possible. Such services should be provided by whoever does it best. Establishing the relative roles of health, social services, voluntary and independent sectors and individuals in determining needs, and funding and delivering services, need to be negotiated and effectively resolved. This has become an ongoing aspect of management in SSDs.

The Structure of the Department

In the light of continuing change, the local authority is currently reviewing the department's structure again. The scale and pace of government policy changes and the results of initial 'Best Value' reviews create a pressure to return to service specialisation and centralisation of management. At the same time, developments in health, such as the introduction of primary care groups, and broader corporate local authority developments still demand that attention be given to issues at a local level. In addition, structures must allow the development of strong inter-organisational relationships, as noted above. The current challenge is to develop both an organisational structure and a managerial approach which are sufficiently flexible to respond to local needs but also promote and maintain internal efficiencies and general consistency of service.

Consistency has both an external and an internal focus. As noted above, the department recognises the need to have a mixed economy of provision and wants to improve the process of contracting to ensure best use of financial resources. In terms of an external focus, the department is working towards greater consistency in contractual arrangements which previously developed in an *ad hoc* manner. The consequence of this *ad hoc* development was variation in costs. The varying patterns of contracting, and different price levels currently negotiated with the independent sector, are anomalous. There is a clear need to be able to demonstrate consistency in conducting relationships with the independent and voluntary sectors. Internally, a key issue is the need to achieve consistency of service delivery across the department. This includes the quality and range of service provided by the department itself.

Developments in home care demonstrate both the current situation and a proposed way forward. Currently, all requests for home care are dealt with in home care teams and it is the manager's role to determine whether the request can be met in-house or whether external purchasing is required. Each team has one identified manager who takes responsibility for working with the independent sector over issues such as development and contract compliance, problem solving and quality assurance. Whilst this has been a relatively successful development, it does not meet the principles of 'Best Value' nor demonstrate consistent practice. A new service organiser role is proposed to deal with these issues. The service organiser would have responsibility for receiving requests, commissioning the service, and dealing with all practical aspects of the contract: that is, payments, queries, quality control and contract compliance. This would also promote better market awareness and gaps could be identified and addressed at local levels. Thus, the department review favours the move away from the existing geographic service provision to a centrally managed model. The current debate revolves around the conditions under which such a model should operate. The particular difficulty here is maintaining consistency whilst promoting the flexibility required to address individual and local needs. The tension between these factors is obvious: centralised models may promote consistency but flexibility and attention to individual need may be neglected as a result.

The 'business unit' model of operating (noted above) would be an approach which would promote flexibility with delegated resources, but this would run counter to a centrally managed model. Additionally, this approach raises issues of a philosophical and practical nature for a local authority. Services are normally accountable through the local government committee process. This unit would require a different model of oversight and accountability, such as a management board. The necessary structural arrangements have yet to be addressed. The department would need to consider how well such an approach would match with its responsibility and accountability to the public and with its tradition of transparency of structure. There is the possibility that a unit could reside in a void, being neither an independent business nor a clear part of the SSD. Additionally, there is the concern of how this model accords with the public service ethos of fairness to those who use and staff the service. Currently, the local authority service is the 'last resort' for users, as it does not have the capacity to refuse or withdraw service from more difficult people. The commitment to vulnerable people must remain. These considerations highlight the complexities of applying commercial principles to public sector organizations (see Potter, 1994).

Staff Development

Staff have been considerably affected by the developments of the last decade and will continue to be so as the pace of change shows no indication of slowing. The task for the department is to maintain a committed group of staff capable of providing high standards of service. However, the changes, which have increased the volume, complexity and importance of administrative and financial work (Harris, 1998), have led many workers to feel de-skilled. Negotiating and maintaining relationships with other service providers is also a continual pressure. There is clear need for continuing professional development to ensure that staff are equipped with the new skills necessary to carry out their roles effectively. In addition, there is increasing pressure to train currently unqualified social care staff. The NVQ programmes noted above are important in promoting a staff culture of learning and development. Managers also need help with adjusting to the new roles and tasks that policy and organizational developments demand of them (DofH/SSI, 1999). All of these issues are of crucial importance, but space here allows only a brief recognition of what is entailed.

Conclusion

In reflecting on the evolution of social care in one SSD, it can be seen that introducing new legislation and revising policy and practice is no simple matter. One theme that has underpinned the account concerns the importance of politics and ideology. The NHS and Community Care Act (1990) was introduced by the Conservative government which was influenced by the principles of New Liberalism. The Labour controlled local authority was unsympathetic to these principles and this is revealed in their uncertainty about the legitimacy of a mixed economy of care. Whilst change inevitably did occur, the authority's approach could be described as minimalist: for example, a coherent strategy to develop and co-ordinate the contribution of commercial and voluntary organisations in the provision of social care services was not initiated. There continued to be a commitment to the principles of the 'classic welfare state' with the

SSD as (almost) sole provider. With a new Labour government in power and a shift in political ideology, already demonstrated in a more agnostic approach to who should provide care, the SSD has been energised to take a more positive approach to both providing and co-ordinating services. However, whilst it is important to note that many of the government's new initiatives have been welcomed, their volume may be a source of stress to already over-stretched SSDs and concerns about the level of funding continue (Hirst, 1999).

Political and ideological principles are not solely at issue. Implementing the mixed economy of care required such a major shift in thinking that time may have been required for the implications to be realised and addressed. Although some theorists have criticised the managerialist influences of recent policy developments in social care (Harris, 1998), the chapter indicates that greater thought and attention has been given to needs of vulnerable elderly people. Organisational change is frequently painful and difficult but over the last decade much advancement has been made in this particular SSD. With the government's constant emphasis on evaluating services and maintaining progress, a continual commitment to change has to be made.

References

Beazley, M. (1994), 'Measuring Service Quality', in Malin, N. (ed.), *Implementing Community Care*, Open University Press, Buckingham.
Butcher, T. (1995), *Delivering Welfare. The Governance of the Social Services in the 1990s*, Open University Press, Buckingham.
Challis, L. (1990), *Organising Public Social Services*, Longman, London.
Cirell, S. and Bennett, J. (1999), *Best Value: Law and Practice*. Sweet and Maxwell, London.
Day, K. (1999), 'Another Piece of the Jigsaw', *Community Care*, 20-26 May, pp. 22-3.
DofH (Department of Health) (1992), *Committed to Quality. Quality Assurance in Social Services Departments*, HMSO, London.
DofH (Department of Health) (1998), *Modernising Social Services. Promoting Independence, Improving Protection, Raising Standards*, The Stationery Office, London.
DofH/SSI (Department of Health/Social Services Inspectorate) (1999), *Modern Social Services – A Commitment to Improve. The 8th Annual Report of the Chief Inspector of Social Services*, Department of Health, London.
Doyal, L. (1993), 'Human Need and the Moral Right to Optimal Community Care', in J. Bornat, C. Pereira, D. Pilgrim, and F. Williams (eds), *Community Care. A Reader*, Macmillan/Open University Press, Basingstoke.
George, M. (1999), 'Cracking the Code', *Community Care*, 22-28 April, pp. 22-3.

Griffiths, R. (1988), *Community Care: Agenda for Action. A Report to the Secretary of State for Social Services*, HMSO, London.
Harris, J. (1998), 'Scientific Management, Bureau-Professionalism, New Managerialism: The Labour Process of State Social Work', *British Journal of Social Work*, vol. 28. pp. 839-62.
Hirst, J. (1999), 'It Hurts, But is it Working?'. *Community Care*, 6-12 May, pp. 6-7.
Kelly, D. and Warr, B. (eds) (1992), *Quality Counts. Achieving Quality in Social Care Services*, Whiting and Birch/Social Care Association, London.
Potter, J. (1994), 'Consumerism and the Public Sector: How Well Does the Coat Fit?', in D. McKevitt and A. Lawton (eds), *Public Sector Management: Theory, Critique and Practice*, Sage, London.

4 New Managerialism and Social Work: Changing Women's Work

ELIZABETH HARLOW

Introduction

There are two main themes running through this chapter. One concerns the way in which new managerialism is affecting both social work organisations and social work practice. Scientific rationality has long been an important concept in management thinking. Today, however, this appears to be increasingly significant. In consequence, social work's traditional concern with the depth and complexity of human emotion is being undermined (Howe, 1996). The increased status of managers and managerial approaches is contributing to an erosion of social work professionalism and autonomy (Dominelli, 1996; Harris, 1998) and a diminution of core values in social work practice. The second theme concerns the gendered nature of social work as an occupation. The development of social work provided women with an opportunity for paid employment and to some extent a career. Hence, the declining status of social work and the changing content of practice particularly impacts upon women. However, the chapter ends with the recognition that women are now less constrained in terms of career opportunities and the changing nature of social work may reduce its appeal.

Women's Work, Men's Work

Philanthropy, the fore-runner of social work, emerged in the transition from feudalism to industrial capitalism. Theorists such as Donzelot (1980) emphasise the part that it played in the new forms of social regulation. However, writers such as Walton (1975), Berg (1978) and Gordon (1989) pay particular attention to the fact that early philanthropists were predominantly women. Whilst participating in a system of social control, these women workers were at the same time attempting to reject another version of control: that is, they were attempting to break out of the domestic confines they had been socially allocated, and take up a role in the public realm. Both Walton and Berg note the resistance that women faced, particularly married women, for attempting to involve themselves in public activities. Hence, many of these women, conscious of conventional gender restrictions and gender inequality, were also members of the early feminist movement (Berg, 1978).

Although it can be argued that these philanthropists were part of the new middle class, and their efforts were still concerned with regulating the poor, Berg claims that it was a sense of commonality and the desire to help other women that motivated their efforts. Thus, according to many feminist accounts, philanthropy was a helping activity predominantly carried out by women and thus feminine (see Chafetz, 1972). Not only this, philanthropy (and later social work) concerned as it was with families and welfare, reflected women's traditional domestic role. As philanthropy transformed into social work, however, a paid occupation for women emerged. Despite the dominant view (as evidenced by marriage bars) that married women should primarily focus their attentions within the home (Walton, 1975), social work provided women with the opportunity of participating in the public sphere and of earning an income.

Whilst philanthropy was a development of women's (often politicised) activity, Walton points out that charity volunteers depended on the financial sponsorship of wealthy men; ecclesiastical leaders, for example. He argues therefore, as does Gordon (1989), that men have always dominated the construction and organisation of philanthropy, and later social work, even though women may have constituted the majority of the practitioners:

> Social work should be the *cause celebre* for women - a profession created by women for women. Yet in reality, women workers operate as the foot soldiers in an army governed by male generals (Rojek *et al.*, 1988, p. 77).

This situation remains the same today. Despite the larger number of women practitioners - the pool from which most managers are promoted (Lawler, 1993) - the management of social work continues to be dominated by men (Howe, 1986; DofH/SSI, 1991; Grimwood and

Popplestone, 1993; see also chapter five in this volume). There are a number of competing explanations of why men are over-represented in management (see Harlow, 1998) but it is not the intention to discuss their relative merits here. Instead, the aim is to explore recent developments with an understanding of social work as a gendered form of employment.

Social work became more fully established as an occupation in Great Britain after World War Two when the welfare state was established. Social workers (mostly women) were employed in the newly created Welfare Departments, Mental Health Departments and Children's Departments. According to Foster (1987), women had gained a number of senior management positions in Children's Departments because this area of work was seen as particularly relevant to them. However, once these three departments were dismantled in favour of unified Social Services Departments, women's representation in senior positions was severely reduced:

> The reorganisation of personal social services in 1971 and subsequent local reorganisation in 1974 decimated the numbers of women in senior positions and effectively ensured a gender revolution which is continuing in a more evolutionary form (Foster, 1987, p. 14).

This trend was also noted by Howe (1986), who explained it in terms of the shift to larger bureaucracies and the attempt to increase the efficient management of welfare services. In order to achieve efficiency it was advocated that the managerial methods of business and industry should be applied (Seebohm Report cited in Howe, 1986). However, this trend, and more specifically the shift towards scientific managerialism, favoured the appointment of men. Howe implies that this can be understood in the following way: rational organisation and scientific managerialism are culturally defined as masculine and, as a result, men may be more willing than women to propose themselves for top management posts and/or those selecting candidates may be more willing to see men as suitable appointments. This was not the first time in the history of social work that a scientific approach was seen as more fitting for men than women. Commenting on a much earlier point in its development, Gordon writes:

> ... the movement they themselves had created now expelled them, as the charity field became professionalised. 'Scientific' charity wanted no

sentimental muddle headed ladies dispensing alms, but tough minded men engaged in long range vision and strategies (Gordon, 1989, p. 65).

The desire for social work organisations to be managed by tough minded managers complete with strategies is even more insistent today. The 1990s has seen a renewed enthusiasm for the application of private sector methods in public organisations. The next section notes recent developments in management thinking in SSDs and highlights the new managerialism that has marked the end of the twentieth century.

Approaches to Management and New Developments in SSDs

The change that followed the Seebohm report led to the increased influence of scientific managerialism. However, its influence was mediated by the human relations approach to management. Whereas scientific managerialism emphasises rationality as a means of most efficiently and effectively achieving the task, the human relations approach includes the principle that attention to workers' emotions and informal work relationships might, in the long run, lead to a more productive outcome. Hollway (1991) argues that the emergence of this school constituted a paradigm shift. She also goes on to argue (Hollway, 1996) that with its emphasis on human need, the approach can be understood as feminine in relation to scientific managerialism. The human relations approach has been particularly relevant in SSDs where, as noted above, managers have been predominantly recruited from the ranks of professionally qualified social workers and this experience has influenced their managerial style. That is, social work practice, traditionally casework heavily influenced by psychodynamic principles, involved skills in working with relationships and the emotional well-being of others. These skills could be transferred into the system of line-management that involved regular one-to-one supervision. Indeed, this system of management was based on the psychodynamic principles that, in order to carry out their work effectively, those on the 'emotional front-line' needed emotional support and assistance themselves.

Hence, the human relations approach was important for both men and women managers. Whilst its importance continues today it has become overshadowed by approaches associated with 'new managerialism': Total Quality Management (TQM) is one example of these new approaches. TQM emanates from private enterprise and is often associated with modern commercial organisations. According to Piggott and Piggott (1992) its foundations lie in both Taylor's scientific managerialism and the human relations school. However, Boje (1996) argues that TQM is only scientific managerialism masquerading as something more. The work of Peters and Waterman (1982) also makes a contribution to new approaches in management. These authors are particularly renowned for focussing on leadership and the way in which organisational values and culture are a crucial means of ensuring excellent quality and organisational success. However, Adams (1998) argues that the new management systems within SSDs do not reflect motivational leadership or the kind of cultural change promoted by Peters and Waterman. Instead, it is the rational objectivity of scientific mangerialism which is most in evidence. Although Newman and Clarke (1994) caution against making simplified claims about the changes in the management in the public sector, it appears that current trends are most heavily influenced by scientific managerialism.

In order to achieve economy, efficiency and effectiveness, modern methods of management used within the private sector have been incorporated into the public sector services (Kelly, 1991). In addition, managers, now more than ever, are expected to use financial objectives to inform policy and practice. This not only means the use of market systems to introduce competition and drive down costs, but also of devolving budget responsibilities to the lowest level possible within the hierarchy. Reducing the number of layers within the organisational hierarchy is also part of this process. This latter strategy is a way of ensuring that all members within the organisation are knowledgeable of, and work within, the strict financial remit.

Increased managerialism also means the certification of management itself. That is, experience of social work practice is no longer seen as adequate for managing social work services: participation in formally accredited training courses for management is now deemed desirable if not essential by employing agencies. Not only this, social work practice experience is no longer viewed as an essential requirement for social work managers: certificated managers can be recruited from outside the service. Although Lawler (1993), examining SSD management in one particular local authority, found no evidence of this practice, later research (Harlow, 1998) found that this does now occur. This development is also noted by Dominelli and Hoogvelt (1996).

As noted above, the introduction of the principles of 'scientific' private sector management into social work is not new. However, these latest developments may lead to new practical implications for women employed as managers or social workers within social work organisations, or women who are the recipients of social services. The issues involved are discussed below.

Implications of New Managerialism

Managers and Careers

Clarke and Newman (1993) argue that the 1980s in general led to the re-making of management. Management development and education became growth fields reinforced through the growing certification process. Indeed management became the driving force for a 'competitively successful society': managers were not only given the right to manage, they were also seen as the new super-heroes. The imagery provided by Clarke and Newman is distinctly masculine; new-managers are seen as cowboys riding in to save the day. Newman (1994), continues this theme. As private sector management has a higher status than public sector management, the introduction of methods from this latter sphere has led to enhanced masculinity, thus increased status and prestige:

> The public sector has so far tended to operate on an image of that (private sector) world as requiring hard, cut-throat, macho or 'cow-boy' styles of working. It is as if the unlocking of the shackles of bureaucratic constraints had at last allowed managers to become 'real men', operating in the 'real world' of the market place, and released from the second-class status of public functionaries (Newman, 1994, p. 194).

The implication of Newman's work is that men would relish these new constructions of public sector management. However, some men and possibly more women may be less enamoured by the changes. Although Keen and Scase's (1996) study of managerialism and middle managers in the public sector does not specifically focus on gender differences, they report that female respondents 'felt their career prospects suffered because of the authority's advocacy of a 'macho' managerial style' (p. 181). This new style and culture which involved, not only notions of 'strong leadership' but also the increased use of militaristic language, was experienced as specifically masculine and uncomfortable.

The introduction of managerialism into the public sector is also associated with an increase in workload due to fewer managers doing more work. This phenomenon led to respondents in Keen and Scase's study reporting a masculine, competitive, workaholic culture which was particularly encouraged by the chief executive. Working long hours was seen as commitment to the organisation. Whilst this culture was resented by both male and female respondents it may be more of an issue for female respondents who are likely to have heavier domestic responsibilities. Similarly, the expectation that staff should acquire management qualifications without secondment would lead to an exhausting burden of work which may create particular difficulties for women. This is not just a practical problem as the demands of work and career are in direct conflict with the emotional investments expected by the dominant constructions of good motherhood (see Harlow, 1998).

The increased volume of work middle managers undertake is accompanied by an increase in responsibility associated with the devolution of authority. Hence, these jobs are more challenging and stressful. Furthermore, the current preference for flatter organisational hierarchies means increased competition for the fewer management jobs that exist. Research suggests that pressured, competitive work cultures are amongst the reasons given for successful women leaving their posts (see Coward, 1992 and Marshall, 1995). Furthermore, the recruitment of managers from outside the social work agency constitutes a lost career opportunity for social workers, most of whom are women. In addition, women social workers may have been happy to become managers if the social work culture, via the human relations approach, had continued upwards throughout the hierarchy. Now, the new management posts may be too far removed from the career upon which they had originally embarked. Or, in Howe's (1986) terms, the scientific managerialism of the new approach may not be conducive to the appointment of women managers.

Despite what might appear to be a series of disincentives, Dominelli (1996) suggests that more women are likely to become managers in the future. She argues that this is, in part, related to the declining status of social work. Subjected to 'dwindling resources and public expenditure cuts' social work becomes ever more difficult. At the same time, its status as a profession is more in question now than ever before (see below). As a result, fewer men will enter as practitioners and there will be fewer men to compete for the available management posts. In addition, management's efforts to maximise women as a human resources will begin to pay off (see DofH, 1992 and Nottage, 1995) and women will be more likely to present themselves for promotion. Whilst Dominelli's speculation may prove to be correct, she does not take into account the above disincentives that may act as a counterbalance.

De-professionalisation

Much of the literature concerned with managerialism and social workers continues the theme identified by Dominelli (1996): that is, recent changes have led to the reduced status of social work and the loss of professionalism. However, by conventional standards social work never achieved full professional status. Aldridge (1996) sets out the arguments on why professional status was never achieved:

- Radical social workers in the 1970s and 1980s resisted professional status on the grounds of its elitism (Bamford, 1990).
- Social workers' emphasis on the use of self and empathy was antithetical to claims of expertise (Aldridge, 1994).
- Because paid work was secondary to the predominantly female work force the incentive to struggle for professional recognition was lacking (Etzioni, 1969; Toren, 1972).
- Feminists argued that professional status was not granted, not because women social workers did not push for it, but because the work involved caring which was a naturally feminine quality and women, therefore, were not seen as needing any reward (Graham, 1983; Witz, 1992).

In keeping with this latter point, Hearn (1982) also identifies social work as a semi-profession because the majority of workers are women. This, argues Hearn (1982), is not because of qualities attributed to women, but because of their status and power in relation to men: that is, female dominated semi-professions such as nursing and social work, service male professions such as law and medicine. Interestingly, Donzelot (1980) made a similar case, and more recently Parton (1991) has argued that following the Cleveland scandal in the late 1980s, the medical profession lost out to the legal profession in defining the content of child care social work. Hearn's thesis has some resonance with the argument that professional status is recognised if the occupation can demonstrate autonomous control (see for example Johnson, 1972 cited in Aldridge, 1996, and Parkin, 1979 cited in Hugman, 1991). Clearly, social workers do not have autonomous control over social services.

This concept is discussed by Clarke and Newman (1993) who argue that the post war welfare state was organised through an 'internal regime of 'professional bureaucracy'':

> By internal regime we mean the articulation of modes of power which connect the structures, cultures, relationships and processes of organisational forms in specific configurations. Both bureaucracy and professionalism involve particular modes of power. They lay claim to particular legitimations for the exercise of power (varieties of expertise and neutrality). They exercise particular ways of deploying power (controlling access to resources or establishing normative judgements). They construct relationships of power between themselves and the recipients of their services (as claimants, clients, patients and so on). The welfare state has drawn together these two modes - bureaucracy and professionalism - in combinations as 'bureau-professional regimes' (Clarke and Newman, 1993, p. 49).

As a result social workers, the majority of whom are state employees, can be understood to be bureau-professionals. According to Clarke and Newman, it was this particular regime of power relations that was seen by the Conservative government in the 1970s to be the stumbling block to efficient, effective and economic public services. As already discussed, managerialism was seen as the answer: politicians, instead of interfering, should get in touch with the real world of 'good business practice'; bureaucrats should become managers and become flexible and outwardly focused; professionals should abandon notions of professional standards and embrace the management culture of efficiency (Clarke and Newman, 1993). Hence, the social work code of ethics becomes increasingly obsolete as organisational managers dictate the day to day practice of social workers (see Banks, 1998).

Harris (1998) is also concerned with the reduction of social work professionalism and professional autonomy. He also acknowledges social workers as bureau-professionals (citing Parry and Parry, 1979) but argues that until the 1980s social workers enjoyed a local autonomy or 'parochial professionalism': that is, in terms of their daily work, social workers could define and prioritise their clients' problems, choose their preferred method of working and organise their time accordingly. Social work supervisors and senior managers did nothing to challenge this arrangement: on the contrary, it was respected and supported. In order for efficiency to be achieved, however, this professional autonomy had to be curtailed and this has been done, says Harris, by an imposition of scientific managerialism. The processes involved are as follows: initially, team leaders should not see themselves as senior social workers, but as managers with a 'business orientation'- devolved budgetary responsibility encourages this; secondly, social workers should have direct responsibility for rationing resources; thirdly, discretionary recording of social work practice is curtailed by computerised systems of standardised recording. On-line recording also by-passes the need for social workers to recount their work in one-to-one supervision sessions; fourthly, social workers' activity and performance is scrutinised by means of information technology:

> ...human and information technology surveillance can be combined with workload measurement integrated into the worker's routine on-line recording. The amount of time needed to manage a caseload can then be determined and managerial attention can be given to 'slow workers'. Supervision sessions can concentrate on the social worker's 'productivity' (Harris, 1998, p. 858).

Supervision sessions do still occur for some workers and there are others (such as Rushton and Nathan, 1996) who continue to advocate a style of supervision which takes into account the social workers' subjective experiences and emotions. However, for many the content of supervision sessions has changed. Instead of providing social workers with the opportunity to reflect, attention is only being given to the mechanics of goals and outcomes. The result is not only the de-professionalisation of social work but also an increase in the anxiety and stress of practitioners (Thompson, 1999).

Social Services and Social Work Practice

The de-professionalisation of social workers is closely connected to the re-definition and fragmentation of social work skills and practice. It has been argued that, as the social work task has become managerialised, social workers have (to some extent at least) become managers themselves (Harris, 1998). Social workers now need to appreciate the costs of services as well as the importance of value for money. New skills are necessary in purchasing and contracting for services (see CCETSW, 1992; 1994) and using information technology. The social worker as manager is most obviously seen in the practice of those working with adults (see Lymbery, 1998) where the job title has been changed to that of care manager. However, the cost of resources is not only an issue for those working in adult services but across the range of services. For example, does a child really need to be accommodated by the local authority and if so what are the cheapest options? Similarly, if the budget for accommodating children is over-spent, then there may be pressure to move children to cheaper placements. This may conflict with goals to limit the moves of children based on evidence that multiple moves are not in their best interests. Hence, there exists the risk that attention to cost over-rules 'professional' considerations concerning the child's emotional well-being. Or, put another way, managerialist priorities dominate professional concerns.

This may be a general trend. Social work practice may focus less attention on the emotional well-being of 'service-users' than ever before. As indicated above, social workers have predominantly become the co-ordinators of services. For the most part, these services are concerned with practical needs. This current model of social work practice contrasts with the preceding model. The casework model attempted to embrace both the emotional and social needs of the individual. The relationship between the worker and the client was crucial: it was a vehicle through which change and progress could be made. Although the casework model was subjected to attack from radicals in the 1970s, some feminists (such as Brown, 1986) argued in favour of its retention on the grounds that it was a feminine approach. It had been developed by women such as Hollis and Perlman who had made an important contribution to the progress of social work. Furthermore, it embraced important nurturing principles. Hence, it should not be lost but critically appraised and built upon.

Today, the direction is away from practice which involves therapy or counselling. Worker-user relationship is only considered in the most superficial sense, if at all (Dominelli, 1996; Harris, 1998; Hopkins, 1996; Howe, 1996):

> Relationships between social workers and clients [have changed] their character from interpersonal to economic, from therapeutic to transactional, from nurturing and supportive to contractual and service-oriented (Howe, 1996, p. 93).

The managerialisation of social work practice means that the relationship to social science knowledge has also changed. Social workers no longer employ sociological or psychological theory in order to reach an analysis of why problems occur but make assessments of presenting behaviours and devise strategies for their management (Howe, 1996). For example, family social workers manage the distress of family members by insisting they keep to allotted roles; probation officers do not try to resolve violent behaviour but rather devise plans for its management. Emphasis is on the here and now and intervention is brief. Goals are achieved as quickly as possible so that cases may be closed and the throughput of work can comply with identified targets. For some, this evacuation of emotional content from practice means that social work has lost its way (see Lousada, 1999). For radicals like Dominelli (1996) it means that social work is losing contact with political movements like feminism as well as its ability to speak up for society's oppressed.

In keeping with the above, social work education does not emphasise critical analysis and the ability to think independently, but rather the acquisition of competencies which have to be performed to a required standard. The social work role has been broken down into specific tasks and the competencies required to perform the tasks have been identified. The acquisition of competencies is assessed by means of performance indicators. Such an approach can be understood as reductionist and behavioural. Once again, all is reduced to outputs which can be objectively quantified and measured. The changes have led to what Jones and Joss (1995) and Dominelli (1996) have described as the Taylorisation of social work. Hence, scientific managerialism has penetrated every corner of social work organisation, management and practice. Critics argue for a more holistic approach to social work and an ongoing reflexive approach to the evaluation of practice (see Jones and Joss, 1995).

It is not the case, however, that current social work practice is without a concern for evaluation, although the emphasis is most usually on official evaluations carried out by organisational managers rather than practitioners qualitatively reflecting on their own work (Shaw and Shaw, 1997). Evaluation is frequently seen in terms of quality assurance, and here we return to an earlier point - the introduction of TQM. Central government may be particularly enthusiastic about quality systems as they enable control to be maintained when responsibilities have been devolved or transferred: that is, by means of inspections, performance targets and guidelines government can continue to influence services for which it has only indirect responsibility. Quality management is summed up as quality assurance:

> According to the Department of Health (DH, 1992a, p26), quality assurance approaches is a catch-all term, including quality control, quality assurance systems and generic quality or total quality. Quality assurance concerns 'all activities and functions concerned with the attainment of quality' (Adams, 1998, p. 13).

One approach to achieving quality is to define the standards of service to be delivered. Such standards can be set locally or nationally. According to Lupton (1992), the government via the Audit Commission and the Social Services Inspectorate (SSI); has been gathering quantitative data on services delivered or made available by local authorities in order to set service norms. Against these service norms the performance of individual SSDs can be judged. However, there is no requirement for the data generated to show how services are relevant to men, women or different ethnic groups. Insensitivity to differences within the population means that the information automatically assumes the perspective of the Anglo-Saxon male. Focussing on gender, Lupton argues that this is the kind of knowledge base that could be expected from a masculine institution:

> One of the central manifestations of a masculinised institutional knowledge-base is the systematic absence of women as a category of knowledge. This invisibility typically originates from, and is compounded by, sex-blind or gender-blind research and information gathering techniques. Sex-blindness occurs most commonly when the process of data collection simply ignores

the sex of the respondent or client as a relevant variable. Without so stratifying the data, however, it is impossible for researchers or policy-makers to assess whether the needs and experiences of women clients are any different from those of male clients, and whether a different kind of service or social work response is consequently needed (Lupton, 1992, p. 96).

Lupton acknowledges the assumption that Local Authorities will supplement the quantitative data required by the SSI or Audit Commission with their own qualitative data. However, she speculates that given the pressure on time and resources, it would be very easy to forego this extra work and rely only on the quantitative data.

The government's approach of standardising services may not in fact lead to an improvement of quality. For example, the imposition of a standard which involves the increase in provision of respite care may be inappropriate for a local authority which has an ethnic population which does not value this service. The provision of services and their evaluation is political, controversial and problematic; values are always implicated and the avoidance of this by means of positivistic quality assurance does not mean the issues will be overcome (Adams, 1998). Such problems are not automatically overcome by an increased emphasis on service users as consumers because the notion of consumer can also be questioned (Dahlberg *et al.*, 1999). Which consumers should be consulted - past, present or future consumers? Is the consumer the direct recipient of the service, such as an elderly person, or the indirect recipient, such as the informal carer of the elderly person? Also, what about the views of tax payers who provide the funds for the services? In addition, argues Dahlberg *et al.*, moral judgements concerning the redistribution of resources come into play. The idea of service users as consumers cannot overcome the problems associated with quality assurance because its foundational principles are flawed:

> Quality is a 'technology of distance', a means of excluding individual judgement and for crossing group and individual borders. Quality cannot be reconceptualised to accommodate complexity, values, diversity, subjectivity, multiple perspectives, and other features of a world understood to be both uncertain and diverse (Dahlberg *et al.*, 1999, p. 105).

Discussion and Conclusion

Taking into account its historical development, it has been argued that social work has provided women with an opportunity of semi-professional employment and (though to a lesser extent) a career in management. The human relations approach allowed managers to continue a welfare oriented approach to their work, although this was always undermined by Taylor's scientific managerialism. More recently, this latter approach has become increasingly significant as it is an influential component of 'new managerialism'. This has implications, not only for managers, but also for social workers and their practice.

According to Clarke and Newman (1993) managerialisation is not just something which has happened in social work. The 1980s and 1990s saw the status of managers raised as management became seen as the solution to a whole manner of organisational and social ills. New managerialism is characterised by an emphasis on success and rationality. It may be seen as a reflection of wider social influences. Lousada (1999) is concerned that the changes in social work reflect a society which is increasingly unable to tolerate the vulnerable, the needy and the dependent. From a psychoanalytical view the emphasis on economy, efficiency and effectiveness in social work may be a way of avoiding having to connect with the experiences of social work clients/service users. The shift away from a case work approach in social work practice can be seen as part of the above trend. Whilst the case work model may have been due for review and the introduction of some managerialist principles may have been appropriate, the recent shifts in social work practice appear to suggest that the baby of emotion and relationship has been thrown out with the bath water of costly inefficiency.

Recent trends have also been identified as a process of de-professionalisation, the result of which is (in part) a reduction in the of status of social workers. Although Harris (1998) suggests that managerialisation has led to social workers becoming managers themselves, their lack of autonomy and the Taylorisation of their role suggest they have become technical workers rather than managers. Given all these changes, will social work and its management remain appealing occupational options for women? The significant decline in applications to social work courses suggests that women are questioning whether social work is for them. This reduced interest may reflect the introduction of tuition fees which might put off mature candidates (Utley, 1998) and/or the attraction of alternative careers. In terms of the latter, the re-location of counselling as a separate specialism or as part of health services offers a different option for women. Also more young women are expressing interest in professions that were previously the exclusive domain of men. Indeed, Higham (1998) warns that in the face of competition from elsewhere social work may struggle to attract high calibre entrants. Initially, philanthropy offered women a role in the public domain. Later, social work offered them paid employment and a career. Now, however, social work is relied upon less for these opportunities. Social work has changed over the years but so have the opportunities afforded women; perhaps even women themselves have changed - that, however, is a topic for another day.

References

Adams, R. (1998), *Quality Social Work*, Macmillan, Basingstoke.
Aldridge, M. (1994), 'Unlimited Liability? Emotional Labour in Nursing and Social Work', *Journal of Advanced Nursing*, vol. 20, pp. 722-8.
Aldridge, M. (1996), 'Dragged to Market: Being a Profession in the Postmodern World', *British Journal of Social Work*, vol. 26, pp. 177-94.
Bamford, T. (1990), *The Future of Social Work*, Macmillan, Basingstoke.
Banks, S. (1998), 'Professional Ethics in Social Work - What Future?', *British Journal of Social Work*, vol. 28, pp. 213-31.
Berg, B.J. (1978), *The Remembered Gate: Origins of American Feminism. The Woman and the City, 1800-1860*, Oxford University Press, New York.
Boje, D. (1996), 'Lessons from Premodern and Modern for Postmodern Management', in G. Palmer and S.R. Clegg (eds), *Constituting Management. Markets, Meanings and Identities*, de Gruyter, New York.
Brown, S. (1986), 'A Woman's Profession', in H. Marchant and B. Wearing (eds), *Gender Reclaimed. Women in Social Work*, Hale and Iremonger, Sydney.
CCETSW (Central Council for Education and Training in Social Work) (1992), *Contracting and Case Management in Community Care: The Challenges for Local Authorities*, CCETSW, London.
CCETSW (Central Council for Education and Training in Social Work) (1994), *Purchasing and Contracting Skills*, CCETSW, London.
Chafetz, J.S. (1972), 'Women in Social Work', *Social Work*, vol. 17, no. 5, pp. 12-18.
Clarke, J. and Newman, J. (1993), 'Managing to Survive: Dilemmas of Changing Organisational Forms in the Public Sector', in R. Page and N. Deakin (eds), *The Costs of Welfare*, Avebury, Aldershot.
Coward, R. (1992), *Our Treacherous Hearts: Why Women Let Men Get Their Way*, Faber and Faber, London.
Dahlberg, G., Moss, P. and Pence, A. (1999), *Beyond Quality in Early Childhood Education and Care: Postmodern Perspectives*, Falmer Press, London.

DofH/SSI (Department of Health/Social Services Inspectorate) (1991), *Women in the Social Services: A Neglected Resource*, HMSO, London.
DofH (Department of Health) (1992), *Promoting Women: Management Development and Training for Women in Social Services Departments*, HMSO, London.
DofH (Department of Health) (1992a), *Committed to Quality: Quality Assurance in Social Services Departments*, HMSO, London.
Dominelli, L. (1996), 'De-professionalizing Social Work: Anti-oppressive Practice, Competencies and Postmodernism', *British Journal of Social Work*, vol. 26, pp. 153-75.
Dominelli, L. and Hoogvelt, A. (1996), 'Globalization and the Technocratization of Social Work', *Critical Social Policy*, vol. 18, no. 47, pp. 45-62.
Donzelot, J. (1980), *The Policing of Families: Welfare Versus the State*, Hutchinson, London.
Etzioni, A. (ed.) (1969), *The Semi-Professions and their Organisation*, The Free Press, New York.
Foster, J. (1987), 'Women on the Wane', *Social Services Insight*, no. 11, pp. 14-15.
Graham, H. (1983), 'Caring: A Labour of Love', in J. Finch and D. Groves (eds), *A Labour of Love*, Routledge and Kegan Paul, London.
Grimwood, C. and Popplestone, R. (1993), *Women, Management and Care*, Macmillan, Basingstoke.
Gordon, L. (1989), *Heroes of the own Lives: The Politics and History of Family Violence, Boston 1880-1960*, Virago, London.
Hall, C. (1992), *White, Male and Middle Class: Explorations in Feminism and History*, Polity Press, Cambridge.
Harlow, E. (1998), 'Gendered Subjectivities: Becoming Managers in a Social Services Department', Unpublished PhD Thesis, University of Bradford.
Harris, J. (1998), 'Scientific Management, Bureau-Professionalism, New Managerialism: The Labour Process of State Social Work', *British Journal of Social Work*, vol. 28, pp. 839-62.
Hearn, J. (1982), 'Notes on Patriarchy - Professionalisation and the Semi-Professions', *Sociology*, vol. 16, no. 2, pp. 184-202.
Higham, P. (1998), 'The Future of Social Work Education in England', Unpublished Paper, Nottingham Trent University.
Hollway, W. (1991), *Work Psychology and Organisational Behaviour. Managing the Individual at Work*, Sage, London.
Hollway, W. (1996), 'Masters and Men in Transition. From Factory Hands to Sentimental Workers', in D. L., Collison, D. L. and J. Hearn (eds), *Men as Managers, Managers as Men. Critical Perspectives on Men, Masculinities and Managements*, Sage, London.
Hopkins, J. (1996), 'Social Work Through the Looking Glass', in N. Parton (ed.), *Social Theory, Social Change and Social Work*, Routledge, London.
Howe, D. (1986), 'The Segregation of Women and their Work in the Personal Social Services', *Critical Social Policy*, vol. 15, pp. 21-35.
Howe, D. (1996), 'Surface and Depth in Social-Work Practice', in N. Parton (ed.), *Social Theory, Social Change and Social Work*, Routledge, London.
Hugman, R. (1991), *Power in Caring Professions*, Macmillan, Basingstoke.
Johnson, T.J. (1972), *Professions and Power*, Macmillan/British Sociological Society, Basingstoke.

Jones, S. and Joss, R. (1995), 'Models of Professionalism', in M. Yelloly and M. Henkel (eds), *Learning and Teaching in Social Work. Towards Reflective Practice*, Jessica Kingsley, London.

Keen, L. and Scase, R. (1996), 'Middle Managers and New Managerialism', *Local Government Studies*, vol. 22, no. 4, pp. 167-186.

Kelly, A. (1991), 'The 'New' Managerialism in the Social Services', in P. Carter, T. Jeffs and M. K. Smith (eds), *Social Work and Social Welfare Year Book 3*, Open University Press, Buckingham.

Lawler, J. (1993), 'The Social Services Manager', Unpublished PhD Thesis, University of Bradford.

Lousada, J. (1999), 'Linking, Thinking and the Future: The Threat to Clinical Social Work and the Attack on Linking', BASW/University of Central Lancashire International Conference Social Work - Making a Difference, 22-25th March, Southport.

Lupton, C. (1992), 'Feminism, Managerialism and Performance Measurement', in M. Langan and L. Day (eds), *Women, Oppression and Social Work. Issues in Anti-discriminatory Practice*, Routledge, London.

Lymbery, M. (1998), 'Care Management and Professional Autonomy: The Impact of Community Care Legislation on Social Work with Older People', *British Journal of Social Work*, vol. 28, pp. 863-78.

Marshall, J. (1995), *Women Managers Moving On. Exploring Career and Life Choices*, Routledge, London.

Newman, J. (1994), 'The Limits of Management: Gender and the Politics of Change', in J. Clarke, A. Cochrane and E. McLaughlin (eds), *Managing Social Policy*, Sage, London.

Newman, J. and Clarke, J. (1994), 'Going about Our Business? The Managerialization of Public Services', in J. Clarke, A. Cochrane and E. McLaughlin (eds), *Managing Social Policy*, Sage, London.

Nottage, A. (1995), 'Women in Social Services. Accelerating the Process of Change', in C. Itzin and J. Newman (eds), *Gender, Culture and Organisational Change. Putting Theory into Practice*, Routledge, London.

Parkin, F. (1979), *Marxism and Class Theory: A Bourgeois Critique*, Tavistock, London.

Parry, N. and Parry, J. (1979), 'Social Work, Professionalism and the State', in N. Parry, M. Rustin and C. Satyamurti (eds), *Social Work, Welfare and the State*, Edward Arnold, London.

Parton, N. (1991), *Governing the Family. Child Care, Child Protection and the State*, Macmillan, Basingstoke.

Peters, T.J. and Waterman, R.H. (1982), *In Search of Excellence*, Harper and Row, New York.

Piggott, J.B. and Piggott, G. (1992), 'Total Quality Management (TQM): The Way Ahead', in D. Kelly and B. Warr (eds), *Quality Counts. Achieving Quality in Social Care Services*, Whiting and Birch/Social Care Association, London.

Rojek, C., Peacock, G. and Collins, S. (1988), *Social Work and Received Ideas*, Routledge, London.

Rushton, A. and Nathan, J. (1996), 'The Supervision of Child Protection Work', *British Journal of Social Work*, vol. 26, pp. 357-74.

Shaw, I. and Shaw, A. (1997), 'Keeping Social Work Honest: Evaluating as Profession and Practice', *British Journal of Social Work*, vol. 27, pp. 847-69.

Thompson, A. (1999), 'High Anxiety', *Community Care*, 1-7 April, pp. 18-19.

Toren, N. (1972), *Social Work: The Case of a Semi-Profession*, Sage, Beverley Hills, CA.
Utley, A. (1998), 'Social Work Left to Flounder by DofE', *The Times Higher Education Supplement*, 22nd May.
Walton, R.G. (1975), *Women in Social Work*, Routledge and Kegan Paul, London.
Witz, A. (1992), *Professions and Patriarchy*, Routledge, London.

5 Equalling the Opportunity of a Management Career

BARBARA DAVEY, PATRICIA KEARNEY AND GWEN ROSEN

Introduction

Although women predominate in the social services workforce, they are under-represented in management, especially in middle and senior positions. This issue has received considerable attention, not least because it is women who are the main providers and users of services and yet policy and decision-making lie primarily with men. It has been pointed out elsewhere that apart from the inequity of this situation, the under-representation of women in management wastes skills and experience and potentially may fail to recognise the needs of women users (SSI, 1991). Despite the implementation of equal opportunities policies and procedures in the 1980s and 1990s, this situation has continued. In 1997, there were 192 social services authorities in the UK, of which 39 were directed by women (SSI, 1997). Within social services, the primary explanations offered for this imbalance are those which emphasise the disadvantages women face because of their caring responsibilities, discrimination in the ways that women are appointed and developed in their careers and the existence of an organisational culture created by and favouring men (SSI, 1991). Generally, discussions of equal opportunities policies centre on trying to address these issues. These arguments are not of course unique to social services and have been put forward to explain the under-representation of women in managerial positions in a variety of professions and organisations, both public and private.

This chapter examines the current position of women in management within the Personal Social Services (PSS) and, specifically, local authority social services departments. It draws on two areas of work undertaken at the National Institute for Social Work (NISW). The first area discusses the evidence from surveys into the working lives and career paths of the social services workforce undertaken by the Research Unit. In particular, this chapter uses evidence from the work histories of the staff in these Workforce Studies to look at the factors associated with attainment of senior positions, in particular the effects of part-time working and qualifications. The studies suggest that men reach senior positions sooner and more often than women, they obtain more qualifications and they work full-time in an environment that rewards full-time more than part-time effort. It has also been argued that in general, one important reason why women have not achieved equality with men is that most women are not as committed to a career (Hakim, 1995). This chapter presents evidence on the career aspirations and the commitment of staff in the Workforce Studies that suggests women and men do not vary in their employment commitment and, in the case of full-time field social workers at least, in their ambitions to manage. We also consider women managers' views of attitudes and practices towards them in their departments.

The second area draws on NISW's work on management and practice development. This area of work includes the Management of Practice Expertise Project, which examined the relationship between professional social care and how it is managed on the front-line. It also draws on a range of consultancy and training programmes, commissioned by agencies in the PSS, that focus on the management and development of front-line practice. These extensive contacts with agencies in the field yield information from women about their career paths and their opinions and experiences as women managers. The development programme provides an opportunity to express the views of practitioners and managers and to give a commentary on the findings from the Workforce Studies. The chapter concludes with some examples of current management practice that aim to negotiate the particular barriers facing women managers in the PSS.

There are a number of ways the material presented in this chapter might be interpreted, three of which are suggested as follows. First, some may reflect the current social structure, and thereby mirror the gendered experiences and attitudes that are formed and demonstrated in other spheres of women's lives. Second, the material may demonstrate the particular working environments of welfare bureaucracies. Third, we suggest that one explanation for the experience of women in social services is that there may be some reflection of the dynamics of care relationships in family and community settings. The key question is how women fare, as traditional carers in a professionalised world of formal care.

The NISW Workforce Studies

Research carried out since 1992 at the National Institute for Social Work has extended our knowledge and understanding of the structure, characteristics and dynamics of the statutory workforce in England, Scotland and Northern Ireland. The research was initiated with three broad aims. The first was to develop an understanding of the structure and dynamics of the workforce, including differences in career patterns between women and men. The second aim was to investigate the experience of working in social services in terms of job satisfaction and stress and the third was to assess developments in training and to investigate the access to training of different groups of staff.

The NISW Social Services Workforce Studies are three pooled longitudinal surveys of social services staff in the UK. The research is based on face-to-face interviews with a stratified random sample of 2,031 employees drawn from the personnel records of five social services departments in England (1,276 respondents), two social work departments in Scotland (393) and all four Health and Social Services Boards in Northern Ireland (362). The study areas were diverse, ranging from an inner London borough to a mainly rural county council, two urban districts in Scotland and a rural and urban mix in Northern Ireland and the findings are generalisable to similar social services departments. The interviews took place in 1993-94 and again in 1995-96, with an interval of between 15 and 24 months between them. Individuals were asked about their current positions and their work histories in social care. The staff occupied the four general occupational categories of manager, field social work staff, residential worker and home care worker. Northern Ireland has a much larger proportion of home care workers in its total workforce than England and Scotland and this group was sampled differently. Therefore, these staff are omitted from this chapter (for details of sampling in the three studies see Balloch *et al.*, 1999). Managers, defined as those with responsibilities for other staff, included strategic and area managers, team leaders, home care organisers and officers in charge of residential homes.

Women and Career Progression

Many studies have shown that women are underrepresented in management positions in a wide variety of public and private organisations. Although women are achieving higher levels of educational qualifications and increasing numbers of women are entering into higher level managerial and professional positions, women are still not reaching the highest echelons of their occupations, including professions where women are concentrated, such as teaching, nursing and social services (Crompton, 1997).

Findings from NHS workforce studies are of particular interest here because similarly to the personal social services, it is a public sector organisation and it employs a majority of women in a 'caring' capacity. In 1991, 80 per cent of NHS employees were women, yet in general management only 18 per cent were women (Donaldson, 1992). Even in the nursing workforce, where men comprise only 7 per cent of the workforce, they are disproportionately represented in management positions. Twelve per cent of community nurse managers, 14 per cent of hospital nurse managers and 37 per cent of nursing officers were men (Seccombe *et al.*, 1993*)*. Davies and Rosser also found than men nurses were promoted to the position of nursing officer much faster that similarly qualified women, even when women had taken no career break. On average, men reached that grade in 8.4 years compared with 17.9 years for women (14.5 years with no career break) (Davies and Rosser, 1986).

Various theories have been offered to explain why women are not reaching management positions in greater numbers. Mainly they have focused on discriminatory processes in the workplace, human capital differences between women and men in the possession of qualifications and experience, and differences between women and men in commitment and ambition. The first has focused on barriers in the workplace where women are subject to discrimination by an organisational culture in which equal opportunities policies are subverted. In a study of social work students in Scotland, three-quarters believed that one reason for there being higher proportions of men than women in social work management is because women are discriminated against by men on the basis of their gender (Taylor, 1994). Other work has focused on how perceptions of roles have served to limit women's advancement. For example, the front-line task of caring is seen as suitable for women whereas management with its function of control is perceived as a role for men (Grimwood and Popplestone, 1993).

The second explanation is based on the differences between women and men in employment patterns which are associated with women's lack of qualifications and work experience and/or their family roles, such as part-time employment and career breaks. Studies investigating the effect of career breaks due to childbearing on occupational mobility have found that the most significant effect is a return to work at a lower level, especially where women resume employment on a part-time basis (Elias and Main, 1982; Stewart and Greenhalgh, 1984; Dex, 1987; Joshi and Newall, 1987). In nursing, part-time working tended to be associated with nurses in lower grades, who showed more dissatisfaction with their career opportunities than full-time staff (Seccombe *et al.*, 1993). Access to training and appropriate qualifications are crucial in the equal opportunities development for women. Jackson and Barber (1993) found that women's family responsibilities adversely affected their ability to attend training courses.

These studies generally refer to women's disadvantaged position in terms of career progression but recently Hakim has suggested that there are many women who are not committed to a career (Hakim, 1995). She has argued that in the analysis of women's under-representation in management, feminists have failed to acknowledge a group of women who choose to prioritise family and home before work and are content to be secondary earners, mainly characterised by working part-time. This group of women are 'uncommitted' to market work unlike women who work full-time. 'Uncommitted' women choose to economise on effort required in market work, namely going on training courses and gaining qualifications because they prioritise home and family. 'Committed' women on the other hand choose to invest in their employment careers. Hakim also maintains that employment careers are not centrally important to most women.

Women continue to be disproportionately responsible for the home and family and many do work part-time to balance domestic responsibilities with paid work. However, commitment to family life does not preclude commitment to paid work and it cannot be assumed that only one commitment is possible, especially in the case of women. A study of women home helps showed they were highly committed to the service they provided even though they prioritised their family responsibilities (Warren, 1990). Secondly, women's aspirations and their working patterns, including their hours of work may vary over the life cycle, depending on their family and caring circumstances and thirdly, women's choices are shaped by available options both in terms of employment and other factors such as availability of good quality child care (Ginn *et al.*, 1996; Ginn and Sandell, 1997). Rubery *et al.*, argue that part-time work is developed generally to suit the requirements of employers rather than those of women (Rubery *et al.*, (1994).

Whether women work full-time or part-time, a lack of desire to move into management is not the same as a lack of commitment to the job. As some writers have pointed out, career is a gendered concept, where the 'male' model of career as full-time, continuous working with progressive upward mobility is considered the norm and any other type of career is considered deficient or inferior in some way (Dex, 1985; Beechey, 1987; Evetts, 1994). Crompton and Sanderson (1990) draw a distinction between organisational/linear careers and practitioner/occupational careers. The former involve promotion to managerial positions and the latter staying in a practice position which may include part-time employment and career breaks. Staying in a practitioner role is one way many women have managed the balance between work and home but it can also represent a positive choice in social services. Many women (and men) find contact with clients a rewarding aspect of their job and may not wish to relinquish this for what may be regarded as managerial, administrative roles. A recent survey of social services staff found that 57 per cent of women and men senior social workers and social workers in the statutory sector had no ambition to become managers (Herbert, 1999). An important consequence of the judgement of career 'success' in terms of the hierarchical model is that the work of those who stay in practitioner roles is often devalued both in terms of status and salary.

In sum, explanations for the disproportionate representation of women in management have focused on gender discrimination, whether real or perceived, and the differences between women's and men's employment patterns which operate to the disadvantage of women, in particular part-time working and career breaks. It has also been suggested that these differences in employment patterns owe less to structural and cultural constraints on women and more to individual preference. We turn now to evidence from the Workforce Studies to examine the factors associated with the attainment of senior positions and discuss differences between women and men in qualifications, hours of work and career breaks. We also discuss the aspirations and commitment of social services staff. Finally, we ask women managers about attitudes and practices they have experienced towards them in their departments to gain a sense of whether they feel they are working in a supportive organisational culture.

Management and Seniority in the Workforce Studies

The Workforce Studies confirmed the predominance of women in each type of job namely manager, field social work, residential work and home care but showed variation in the degree of predominance. In England, for example, women comprised 86 per cent of the total workforce, 78 per cent of field social workers, 85 per cent of residential workers, 96 per cent of home care workers yet only 65 per cent of managers (Balloch et al., 1999).

Ginn examined the work histories of respondents since their first job in social care to explore the influence of gender on occupational attainment. She created the concept of 'seniority' as a broader category than manager to identify those staff who had reached a position of managerial responsibility within their field of work. This category included team leaders and senior social workers, home care organisers and managers, and officers in charge and managers in residential homes (Ginn et al., 1997). Seniority will be discussed within the occupational categories of social work, home care and residential work and central and strategic managers.

Table 5.1 shows differences between women and men in seniority in all geographical areas. For example in England, 38 per cent of men field social work staff were senior compared to only 12 per cent of women. In Northern Ireland, 41 per cent of men field social work staff were senior compared with 20 per cent of women. Central and strategic managers with responsibility for planning and managing the agency as a whole are included as a separate column and are shown as a percentage of all staff. In England, only 1 per cent of women are represented at this level compared with 8 per cent of men. There are similar proportions in Scotland to England and in Northern Ireland, 20 per cent of men are represented at central and strategic level compared with only 4 per cent of women staff.

Having established the differences between women and men in the achievement of seniority, other factors were explored which were expected to be associated with promotion in social services. These included age, professional and educational qualifications and hours of work in the current job. Past employment patterns, namely age of entry into social care and social services, length of service, number of jobs held, number of years spent in full and part-time working and length of career breaks were also examined. Logistic regression was used to identify the statistically significant factors associated with the probability of being in a senior post when all these variables were taken into consideration. This analysis was undertaken separately for each of the occupational categories in all three study areas (see Ginn and Buglass, 1996; Ginn et al., 1996; Ginn et al., 1997 for details). Before discussing these findings, we look briefly at the differences between women and men in qualifications, hours of work and career breaks.

Table 5.1 Percentages of staff who were senior by occupational category and gender

	Social work		Home care		Residential work		Central	
	Women	Men	Women	Men	Women	Men	Women	Men
England	21	38	4	16	7	16	1	8
Scotland	12	31	3	23	3	8	1	8
Northern Ireland	20	41	-	-	10	34	4	20

Source: Ginn and Fisher, 1999, p. 131

Women were less likely to be qualified than men. In the three studies overall, at first interview, 51 per cent of women managers compared with 77 per cent men held a CQSW, DipSW or CSS qualification. In the case of social work staff, these figures were 73 per cent of women and 85 per cent men (Andrew, 1999). Holding a professional qualification increased the likelihood of seniority in all occupational categories except home care in all study areas. Even when qualified, however, women on average had taken longer to reach their first senior position than men. In the case of senior social work staff in England, the mean time from qualifying to first senior position was 8.7 years for women but 6.6 years for men.

Career breaks and part-time working are among the suggested reasons for women's under-representation in management. Our data show that nearly all men in the social services worked full-time but about half of all women worked part-time. In England 10 per cent of men worked part-time compared with 50 per cent of women. In Scotland, only 4 per cent of men worked part-time compared with 51 per cent of women and in Northern Ireland no men worked part-time but 11 per cent of women managers, field social work staff and residential workers did. There was wide variation between job types. In England, for example, part-time working was least common among women managers (5 per cent), followed by social work staff (19 per cent). The proportion rose to 35 per cent among women residential workers and to 76 per cent of home care staff (Balloch and McLean, 1999). Staff employed full-time were more likely to hold a senior position than those working part-time. Analysis also indicated that the seniority was associated with number of years spent in full-time work but not part-time.

Since their first job in social services, overall one in ten women in management and social work had taken a career break to spend time caring for the family in the three samples. No men gave family responsibilities as a reason for taking a career break. Reporting career breaks for maternity leave was more complex. For example, a third of women in social work had a baby in a year *after* first joining social services yet only 7 per cent reported taking paid maternity leave which may suggest women took unpaid maternity leave or that women did not view maternity leave as a career break (Andrew, 1999).

When all variables were included in the regression models, once work history and qualification factors were taken into consideration gender was *not* a significant factor in the achievement of seniority. This suggests that women are not discriminated against directly. Length of full-time service in social care was a major predictor of the likelihood of being in a senior post in all occupational categories and in all areas, the only exception being residential work in Northern Ireland. Years of part-time service made no apparent contribution.

Other factors associated with seniority were as follows. In field social work, holding a professional qualification was only significant in Northern Ireland. Higher educational level was associated with attaining seniority in field social work in England. In residential work, holding a professional qualification was significant in all three geographical areas and in Northern Ireland, it was the only factor. In home care in England and Scotland, in addition to length of full-time service, a greater number of jobs also contributed to achievement of seniority. In central and strategic management, higher educational levels were associated with seniority in England and Northern Ireland whereas in Scotland, a professional qualification contributed to seniority but a higher educational level did not do so.

These are initial findings and the data are subject to continuing analyses that take into account factors such as staff who had not yet reached a senior position but may do so in the future, as well as the timing of events. Therefore caution should be used in making causal inferences. These analyses imply that women are not discriminated against directly but are disadvantaged in career progression because of their shorter average full-time experience coupled with lower educational and professional qualifications. However, even qualified women took longer on average to reach seniority than did equivalently qualified men. In addition, length of part-time service in social care appears to have no influence on achievement of seniority suggesting that part-time jobs are not seen to provide adequate experience for promotion.

Career Aspirations

There have been suggestions that women are not as ambitious or committed to a career as men, although as discussed earlier the definition of 'career' has been questioned. We asked the non-managers in the survey whether they would be interested in becoming a manager (defined as manager of staff). In the three studies overall, 57 per cent of field social work staff, half of residential workers and one-third of home care staff were interested in going into management. Figure 5.1 shows the differences between women and men in all three occupational categories.

Overall, 70 per cent of men said they were interested in going into management compared with 43 per cent of women. Figure 5.1 shows these differences as two thirds of men compared with just over half of women in field social work, and 71 per cent of men compared with just under half of women residential workers. Only one-third of women home care workers were interested in going into management of staff. In residential work and home care, there were virtually no differences between women who worked part-time and those who worked full-time in management aspirations. In field social work, however, just under two thirds of women working full-time said they were interested in going into management compared with one-third of women working part-time. The data suggest then that whether staff work full or part-time there are differences between women and men in management aspirations in residential work and home care. In field social work, however, there are virtually no differences in management aspirations among women and men who worked full-time but fewer women part-time workers are interested in promotion. This is an area that requires further exploration.

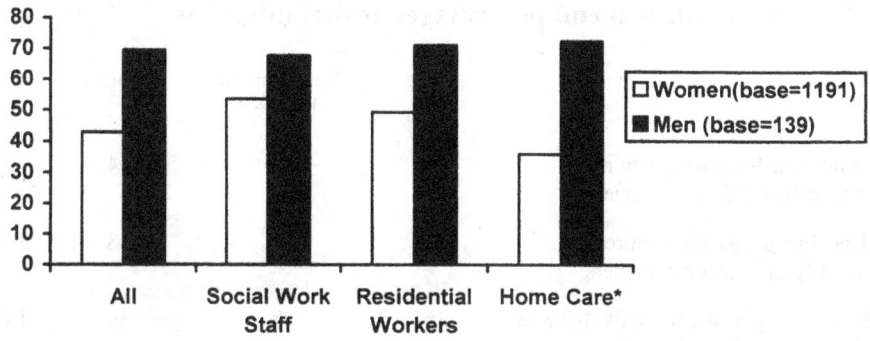

*does not include Northern Ireland. Numbers are small for men home care workers

Figure 5.1. Percentage of staff interested in management of staff by gender

In the Community Care Survey, both women and men social workers gave budget pressures, too much responsibility and too little contact with clients as some of the reasons for their desire not to go into management (Herbert, 1999). Women may also wish to stay in a practitioner role because they perceive gender discrimination in achieving promotion, a finding in Taylor's (1994) study of social work students. In that study, 59 per cent of women students compared with 4 per cent of men thought that their chances of promotion would be detrimentally affected by their gender. Half of the men compared with 16 per cent of the women thought that their chances would be positively enhanced by their gender. Of course, this is not particular to the social services workforce. Jackson and Barber's (1993) survey also found that women NHS staff felt that despite their commitment to work and career progression, they would have to overcome additional career barriers.

The perceptions among women of an unfavourable workplace culture could deter them from seeking promotion, especially if this is the feeling of women managers themselves. In the Workforce Studies, we asked women managers at both interviews questions relating to attitudes and practices towards them.

Table 5.2. Women managers' perceptions of attitudes and practices towards them: percentages at first interview

	Agree	Neither agree nor disagree	Disagree	Base
Males managers are given more respect than female managers	44	22	34	197
The climate has been improving recently for women managers	53	29	18	197
Male managers are more likely to be allocated responsible work	36	28	36	197
Women managers tend to find themselves in a marginal position	43	24	33	197

Table 5.2 shows that at first interview sizeable numbers of women managers in the three countries, with some variation, perceive a workplace culture where men receive more respect and women managers are marginalised, although more than half felt the climate was improving. There was little overall change at second interview.

Management ambitions are not the same as commitment. To gain a sense of the employment commitment of staff, individuals were asked about their readiness to stay in work if they had enough money to live comfortably for the rest of their lives. In the English study, similar proportions of women and men, just over half, would stay in work. There were no differences between part-time and full-time staff except in field social work, where 41 per cent of full-time staff would give up work but only 20 per cent of part-time workers (McLean, 1995).

The data suggest that there are differences between women and men in career ambition, if this is defined as aspirations to manage staff, except for full-time field social workers. However, there are no differences between men and women in employment commitment. One reason for women not wishing to become managers could be the perception of an unfavourable workplace culture and indeed a sizeable minority of women managers finding themselves in a marginal position. The chapter now turns to NISW's development work to provide some suggestions for these findings. This work is also used to discuss some reasons for the longer time taken for women to achieve career progression and the role of part-time working in management and training. Finally, we conclude with some suggestions as to how some of the problems raised can be negotiated.

Commentary from Development Work at NISW

The Workforce data show that men reach management posts sooner than women. Women staff taking part in NISW's development work give two main reasons for this longer time taken for career progression. Firstly, some women consider they need a strong practice grounding before seeking promotion and sometimes think that male colleagues are promoted without sufficient fundamental experience. It may be the case that women apply for a more senior post when they are confident it is within their ability whereas men apply for positions where they can learn new skills. Secondly, some women consider that they are more likely to obtain a higher post in another organisation rather than within their own. There may be a number of factors at play here. Presumptions about ambition and how it is expressed can mean that an organisation retains a competent woman in her current post but does not regard her as potential for promotion. Women are often less mobile than men in the workforce (Andrew, 1999) and so are less likely to work their way out of this particular difficulty. Neither of these notions is particular to the social services workforce but the lack of workforce planning and professional development frameworks within local government, still a major PSS employer, are likely to reinforce these attitudes and practices.

The Workforce Studies found that length of part-time working made no apparent contribution to the probability of achieving seniority. For a range of reasons, women are less likely to work full-time for long periods than their male counterparts. Part-time workers are considered unsuitable for a number of management posts in social service departments. This may be a phenomenon specific to social work agencies, since elsewhere in local authorities, job shares and part-time sessional working are much more common activities among other professional staff, for example, surveyors and lawyers.

In our development work with senior women at assistant director level and above, participants discussed the ways in which there is an assumption that all senior posts are full-time. Yet in practice there are hardly any jobs that could not be part-time or job share. Senior women also described an organisational culture that assumes that *more* than a full-time presence is needed to demonstrate commitment. British managers work the longest hours in Europe but it is questionable whether this makes them more effective or productive than their European counterparts. Part-time, term-time workers and job sharers are often perceived as lacking commitment to the organisation and the task. Another area where part-time workers in Personal Social Services agencies can be disadvantaged is in access to training and development opportunities. We have found that there seems to be an over-representation of men selected for development, a process which merits closer examination. Furthermore, training and development courses are, in our experience, rarely timetabled to allow for full participation by part-time workers.

The Workforce data suggest that there are no differences between women and men full-time social workers in their desire to become managers. Further analysis is required to establish whether these ambitions go beyond first-line level management, where women are better represented, to more senior management. First-line managers manage teams of practitioners, and their central task is to develop and support the collective practice of their team. This may be doubly meaningful for women at work. It allows a career move that is still obviously focused on practice but it may be a further example of the perceived care rather than control aspects of management (Grimwood and Popplestone, 1993). In our experience in development work within agencies, we find that many women make a conscious decision to go no further. In other professions, advancement into management is not synonymous with relinquishing a professional identity. Nurses, doctors, solicitors and teachers can still retain their professional practice to varying degrees. Field social workers, particularly in statutory agencies, do not all welcome the invitations to become a manager. This may be a variation on the expressed wish of many women in practitioner roles to retain their professional practice base.

The direct tasks of supervision and team leadership may offer women a more attractive management role than senior management posts appear to do. Management philosophy of the 1990s promoted the theory that a competent manager could manage any organisation (Pollitt, 1993).

This led to senior services managers in particular becoming detached from social work practice, its particular and unique special knowledge, skills and theoretical issues.

Changing the Culture

The Workforce data have also suggested that many women managers perceive workplace culture as unfavourable to them. A further point is that men predominate in senior management posts in social care agencies and they therefore make up the majority of interview panels and appointment decisions. The phenomenon of like employing like is suggested in many areas of work. Therefore assumptions about the nature of competence and commitment may favour male candidates.

Discussion about equal opportunities for women advocates 'cultural change'. We suggest that 'culture' is a kaleidoscope of circumstances and, in this context, is helpfully understood to mean tradition and current custom and practice. Therefore, change will require a variety of activities. We note some of the manifestations of the status quo and how they might be addressed:

- *Formal initiatives*: these will mean that the organisation legitimises and analyses the particular needs and difficulties experienced by women in the workforce, which can then be translated into a range of structural changes allowing flexible and 'carer-friendly' practice. Some of these are discussed below and for a fuller discussion of such initiatives see Institute of Personnel Management (1990).

- *Management development programmes* that incorporate this analysis, through both women-only and mixed forums. Women report favourably on the opportunity for women-only forums: 'The views that women workers express in confidential interviews would have been hard, if not impossible, for them to convey directly to their more senior managers' (Nottage, 1995, p. 188) and is echoed in the experience of the LGMB Women's Leadership Programme: 'For the majority of participants ... the 'women only' aspect of the programme was significant - with the learning environment described as safe, supportive, open and encouraging' (Wills, 1997 p. 16). However, gender issues also inform all management development activity, both to raise general awareness and to allow the 'carer-friendly' approach to be articulated and applied to men and women workers. This allows the organisation to consider the implications of male and female approaches to work:

> Every woman interviewed, with or without children or other caring responsibilities, understood the need to establish the domestic context of the working life. The responses of male managers to a question about their personal circumstances varied. Some were prepared to admit to having children. Others found this line of questioning invasive and outside the remit of the interview. One senior manager complained 'You're asking very personal questions. What has this to do with my work?' (Holly, 1998, p. 62)

- *Critical mass*: The lack of women in senior management means there are few positive role models for women. Women managers have told us of the informal mentoring arrangements that have helped them. We have found few instances where these arrangements are a formal part of management development programmes. Organisations that support these arrangements give their women managers confidence and skills. Where women are a minority at senior management level, they can experience a paradoxical effect of tokenism:

> Women senior managers do get tired of having to fight their corner: 'I don't want to turn into the woman who is always bleating and moaning about how women are treated. I want to be listened to with respect and not greeted with a sigh or boredom every time I raise equality issues' (Holly, 1998, p. 70-71).

- *Senior management modeling good practice*: these groups are predominantly male, and may remain so for some time. They are able to have a powerful effect on changing the status quo by their behaviour. This inevitably means looking at personal attitudes to women's roles, which may mirror more general social attitudes to women at work as demonstrated by a recent industrial tribunal:

> Sheila Toon, a 51-year-old airline secretary-administrator, resigned last year after being put on a rota to carry out hostess duties at management meetings. She then took her employer to an industrial tribunal for sex discrimination and constructive dismissal. Toon

describes her former role as 'assistant manager' and says she 'ran the department when the manager was absent'. Apart from the fact that she felt insulted, she was convinced it would be counter-productive for both her and her department manager to be absent at the same time, which would have happened if the rota was enforced. The airline's case appeared to be weakened when it admitted that one of its female managers had joined the hostess rota. When asked to account for this, the feeble explanation was that this manager used to be a secretary before she was promoted. It does not seem to have occurred to the male managers that they could pass round sandwiches themselves (*The Guardian*, 5.7.99).

Whilst such employment practices may look increasingly arcane, they have a particular resonance within social care agencies, where the roles of women as carers and service users will be of continuing interest. Within local authorities:

> ...there were concerns raised by both women managers and non-managers about the way some male managers relate to female non-management staff...There are also comments made to women attending meetings specifically for female staff: We had a women's meeting and the male senior manager said 'Are you off to your women's knitting bee now?' (Holly, 1998, p. 68-9).

McDougal and Briley conclude that:

> The notion of changing managerial assumptions about women in management is one which should not be underestimated. It is a strategy which challenges beliefs and values, many of which have their routes in the socialisation process, and therefore is likely to be met with considerable resistance (1994, p. 25).

Aspirations and Advancement

The Workforce Studies data show that men reach management posts sooner and more often than women, they obtain more qualifications and they work full-time in an environment that rewards full-time more than part-time effort. This is particularly so regarding advancement and opportunities for professional development. That some women work part-time because of family and caring responsibilities does not necessarily indicate a lack of commitment to paid work, borne out by the finding that fewer part-time than full-time workers say they would stop work if they had enough money to live comfortably. Rather, this suggests that part-time working is a way of balancing the dual commitments of work and family. Reasons for differences between women and men in aspirations to manage require further investigation. For women working part-time, the deficiency of part-time management posts could be a factor. Among full-time field social workers, there were no differences between women and men in management ambitions, although they may mean very different things by management. We have given some possible reasons for the disparity between women and men in senior management posts. We suggest that 'management', 'advancement', 'commitment' and 'competence' may be operating as gendered concepts. Thus, if full-time, continuous working with progressive upward mobility is regarded as the norm, then anything other than this can be seen as 'failing'. Moreover, any different career path is likely to be underestimated for the other kinds of experience and skills it brings. This raises three questions. How might women be afforded the same opportunities as men? Do we have anything to learn from the different experience and expertise that women bring to the workforce? How can this be used to inform practice and service development?

There seems no reason, other than custom and practice, why training and development opportunities should not be as available to part time as they are to full-time workers. All staff need to know how to do their job as well as possible and be prepared for the changes that are a constant feature of work in the Personal Social Services. Flexible arrangements for professional development offer the means to do this, through work-based learning programmes that can plan around work-timetables and through accreditation of prior experience, which not only allows part-time effort to be counted, but can consider a variety of experience as enriching. Women practitioners and managers in particular describe the difficult balancing they do in managing caring responsibilities and work responsibilities. Complex decisions are made daily and in the longer term in relation to caring for children, parents and other dependent relations. Decisions about workplace, education or training are made in relation to caring responsibilities. Taking work where you can find it, rather than following the job, may provide wider relevant experience than is afforded by a conventional career path. Balancing care and work responsibilities may make you a skilled time manager and good at complex problem solving (Knight, 1994). All of these are useful abilities for a manager in any organisation.

Training arrangements can be developed to benefit all staff and varied work experience can offer valuable management skills. However, these both depend on attitudinal change throughout the workforce: varied career paths will need to be accepted as equivalent successes to the current norm, not failures. Employers will need to re-consider arrangements that assume staff in part-time posts are not interested in personal and professional development.

Practice-based Definitions of Management

Many women and surely men also, may decide not to take on more senior management posts because of the perception that caring and controlling require different and gender specific abilities. We will consider below how workers might usefully challenge such distinctions. However, practitioners and first-line managers rarely get the opportunity to test out their assumptions since their spheres of action and those of senior managers rarely coincide. Where agencies have attempted to link the two, we have found a different picture. Agencies that invite staff to observe senior management meetings, to shadow and to be mentored by senior colleagues report benefits for both groups of staff. These initiatives open up an otherwise tightly closed activity but require a confidence and transparency from senior managers that they may find difficult to undertake. In our experience, these instances are more often set in motion by innovative individual senior staff, often women who have reflected on the difficulties of their own career progression. They are less likely to be a formal, agreed and resourced part of the agency's workforce planning and management development processes. These processes are in their infancy it seems, in many agencies in the PSS. Social service departments are facing a recruitment crisis: applications to social work courses have dropped 50 per cent over the past three years and the ADSS notes that:

> ...the fact is that posts just cannot be filled. People need help and the money is there to pay for it. But people of the right quality are just not coming forward for recruitment (*The Guardian*, 14.7.99).

More flexible working arrangements, reflecting the needs of the majority of the Personal Social Services workforce, can play a significant part in recruitment and retention initiatives.

Similarly, we have found that agencies used to undertaking planning and development work across hierarchy levels offer staff creative opportunities for working with senior colleagues, seeing them in action and most importantly, making their own contribution to the strategic working of the organisation. Such 'vertical slice' activity is not common, however, and strategic activity is often confined to designated sections, isolated from the organisation's operational mainstream.

Some of the perceived notions about the split between care and control may be accurate: the tension between managing the practice and managing the department is one that has been commented on extensively (see NISW (1995) for further discussion of these issues). The Personal Social Services, like other human services organisations have been greatly affected by the imposition of managerialism throughout the 1980s and 1990s (Pollitt, 1993). Under current Government requirements local authorities are trying to integrate best management practice within the context of user defined service delivery and professional values and expertise. We suggest that it may be helpful to think of the concept of 'management' as a gendered one with some fairly basic distinctions attesting practitioners as 'caring', and managers as 'controlling'. There is a need to challenge such assumptions, including the contradictions they contain. Where, in this framework, is there room for the practitioner's autonomy and judgement or for the manager to lead practice? How are the vital connections between managing front-line practice and managing the department to be understood and sustained for the benefit of service users?

We suggest that the adequate representation of women at senior management levels in the Personal Social Services is important for a number of reasons. Women are entitled to equivalent opportunities to men. These opportunities may well be different from the career paths that are currently given value and status. We would expect organisational cultures to be modified if the proportion of women and men in management reflect those of the population served and of the workforce employed.

Exploring issues of gender leads us to re-consider the nature of management within the Personal Social Services. Addressing inequities between women and men should in turn promote some fundamental thinking about the nature of welfare and its delivery. Dealing with difference lies at the heart of welfare provision in our society: the role of women within the workforce gives us the opportunity to consider the essential elements of our business.

References

Andrew, T. (1999), 'Employment History of Social Services Staff' in S. Balloch, J. McLean and M. Fisher (eds), *Social Services: Working Under Pressure*, Policy Press, Bristol.
Balloch, S., Andrew, T., Ginn, J., McLean, J., Pahl, J. and Williams, J. (1995), *Working in the Social Services*, NISW, London.
Balloch, S. and McLean, J. (1999), 'The Changing Nature of Work', in S. Balloch, J., McLean and M. Fisher (eds), *Social Services: Working Under Pressure*, Policy Press, Bristol.
Balloch, S., McLean, J. and Fisher, M. (eds) (1999), *Social services: Working Under Pressure*, Policy Press, Bristol.
Beechey, V. (1987), *Unequal Work*, Verso, London.
Crompton, R. (1997), *Women and Work in Modern Britain*, Oxford University Press, Oxford.
Crompton, R. and Sanderson, K. (1990), *Gendered Jobs and Social Change*, Unwin Hyman, London.
Davies, C. and Rosser, J. (1986), *Processes of Discrimination: A Study of Women Working in the NHS*, DHSS, London.
Dex, S. (1985), *The Sexual Division of Work*, Wheatsheaf, Brighton.
Dex, S. (1987), *Women's Occupational Mobility: a Lifetime Perspective*, Macmillan Press, London.
Donaldson, L. (1992), 'Some Women Are More Equal Than Others', *Independent*, 5 November.
Elias, P. and Main, B. (1982), *Women's Lives: Evidence from a National Training Survey*, Institute for Employment Research, Coventry.
Evetts, J. (ed.) (1994), *Women and Career: Themes and Issues in Advanced Industrial Countries*, Longman, Harlow.
Ginn, J., Arber, S., Brannen, J., Dale, A., Dex, S., Elias, P., Moss, P., Pahl, J., Roberts, C. and Rubery, J. (1996), 'Feminist Fallacies: A Reply to Hakim on Women's Employment', *British Journal of Sociology*, vol. 47, no. 1, pp. 169-74.
Ginn, J. and Buglass, D. (1996), *Working in Social Work Departments in Scotland*, NISW, London.
Ginn, J. and Fisher, M. (1999), 'Gender and Career Progression', in S. Balloch, J. McLean and M. Fisher (eds), *Social Services: Working Under Pressure*, Policy Press, Bristol.
Ginn, J., McConkey, W. and McLean, J. (1996), *Working in the Social Services in Northern Ireland - An Analysis of Work Histories*, NISW, London.

Ginn, J., McLean, J., Andrew, T. and Balloch, S. (1997), *Work Histories of Social Services Staff*, NISW, London.

Ginn, J. and Sandell, J. (1997), 'Balancing Home and Employment: Stress Reported by Social Services Staff', *Work, Employment and Society*, vol. 11, no. 3, pp. 413-34.

Grimwood, C. and Popplestone, R. (1993), *Women, Management and Care*, BASW/Macmillan, Basingstoke.

Hakim, C. (1995), 'Five Feminist Myths about Women's Employment', *British Journal of Sociology*, vol. 46, no. 3, pp. 429-55.

Herbert, S. (1999), 'Stress among Front-line Workers is Overwhelming, Reveals Survey', *Community Care*, 29 April–5 May, p.1.

Holly, L. (1998), 'The Glass Ceiling in Local Government: A Case Study', *Local Government Studies*, vol. 24, no. 1, pp. 60-73.

Institute of Personnel Management (1990), *Work and the Family: Carer-friendly Employment Practices*, IPM National Committees for Equal Opportunities and Pay and Employment Conditions, IPM, London.

Jackson, C. and Barber, L. (1993), *Women in the NHS: Experiences in South East Thames*, Institute of Manpower Studies, Brighton.

Joshi, H. and Newall, M.L. (1987), 'Job downgrading after childbirth', in M. Uncles (ed.), *London Papers in Regional Science 18. Longitudinal Data Analysis: Methods and Applications*, PION, London.

Knight, J. (1994), 'Motherhood and Management', in M. Tanton (ed.), *Women in Management: A Developing Presence*, Routledge, London.

McDougall, M. and Briley, S. (1994), *Developing Women Managers : Current Issues and Good Practice*, HMSO, Edinburgh.

McLean, J. (1995), 'The Experience of Working in the Social Services', in S. Balloch, J. McLean and M. Fisher (eds), *Working in the Social Services*, NISW, London.

Nottage, A. (1995), 'Women in Social Services: Accelerating the Process of Change' in C. Itzin and J.J. Newman (eds), *Gender, Culture and Organisational Change: Putting Theory into Practice*, Routledge, London.

NISW (National Institute for Social Work) (1995), *The Great Divide: Managing Practice or Managing the Department*, Collected Conference Papers, NISW, London.

Pollitt, C. (1993), *Managerialism and the Public Services: The Anglo-American Experience*, Blackwell, Oxford.

Rubery, J., Horrell, S. and Burchell, B. (1994), 'Part-Time Work and Gender Inequality in the Labour Market', in A.M. Scott (ed.), *Gender Segregation and Social Change*, Oxford University Press, Oxford.

Seccombe, I., Ball, J. and Patch, A. (1993), *The Price of Commitment: Nurses Pay, Careers and Prospects*, Institute of Manpower Studies, Brighton.

SSI (Social Services Inspectorate) (1991), *Women in Social Services: A Neglected Resource*, HMSO, London.

SSI (Social Services Inspectorate) (1997), *Training Support Programme: a Report on Targets and Achievements in 1995/6*, Department of Health, London.

Stewart, M. and Greenhalgh, C. (1984), 'Work History Patterns and the Occupational Attainment of Women', *Economic Journal*, vol. 94, pp. 493-519.

Taylor, C. (1994), 'Is Gender Equality in Social Work Management Relevant to Social Work Students?', *British Journal of Social Work*, vol. 24, pp. 157-72.

Warren, L. (1990), 'We're Home Helps Because We Care: The Experience of Home Helps Caring for Elderly People', in P. Abbott and G. Payne (eds), *New Directions in the Sociology of Health*, Falmer Press, London.

Wills, J. (1997), 'Kicking Down the Barriers', *Local Government Management Board*, Summer, LGMB, London.

SECTION TWO

INTERNATIONAL PERSPECTIVES

6 Crossing, Building and Breaking the Boundaries: Social Work in a Global Context

LIAM HUGHES

Introduction

Previous chapters in this volume have concentrated on UK developments in the organization, management and practice of social work. However, there is also an increasing need to appreciate national arrangements in a wider international context. It is the goal of this chapter to highlight the broader picture. This does not mean that all relevant issues will be addressed: all that can be achieved is an introduction to some of the main considerations and debates.

In the first section of the chapter attention is drawn to arguments concerning the impact of the global economy on social policy in general, and the organization of social welfare in particular. Boundaries between nation states are being re-defined in response to economic and political changes. Europeanisation is now on the agenda. This refers to the breaking down of barriers between states in Europe, and it can be seen as an example of the regionalisation which, according to Wilding (1997) results from globalisation. The tension between the strengthening of regional boundaries and the increasing permeability of national boundaries is an increasingly important issue.

Despite the growing emphasis on international competition, there are some trends leading towards a common European approach to social policy. Attention is particularly drawn to the increasing importance of the concept of social exclusion. Concern with ensuring that all members of society are included relates again to boundaries. However, efforts to include do not always extend beyond the boundaries of the EU itself as tough approaches to immigration have led some commentators to suggest that Fortress Europe is being built. Following this, the question of whether there is potential for a universal approach to social work and social care is addressed. This penultimate section brings to the fore the (apparent) paradox that, whilst global influences are in play, attempts to universalise notions of social work and social care are undermined by the postmodern focus on diversity and the enduring importance of the local. The chapter concludes with a return to some of the major questions concerning globalisation.

Breaking Global Boundaries

> Globalization has become a fashionable concept in the social sciences, a core dictum in the prescriptions of management gurus, and a catch-phrase for both journalists and politicians. It is widely asserted that we live in an era in which the greater part of social life is determined by global processes, in which national cultures, national economies and national borders are dissolving (Hirst and Thompson, 1996, p. 1,195 cited in Cope, 1999, p. 47).

> [Globalisation is] a shorthand description of the internationalization of production, capital flows and markets, the emergence of transnational and supernational agencies and the internationalization of culture. The changes are economic, political and social (Wilding, 1997, p. 411).

The perception that we live in a globalised world has been at the centre of recent political and economic debate. There is widespread agreement that this is also related to innovations in communications and transport, and to changes in contemporary capitalism. The domination of a global economy has led some to argue that nation states are being undermined: they are being 'hollowed out'. That is, they are increasingly less able autonomously to control what goes on within their boundaries (McGrew, 1992). Although the extent is debated (see below), it is generally agreed that globalisation has some impact upon the economic policies that are pursued, the nature of social life, the problems that emerge and the kind of welfare policies that individual states follow. If the globalisation hypothesis is correct, we should anticipate greater convergence in public policies amongst the advanced welfare states because no individual government could afford to be too far out of line on economic and environmental regulation, rates of taxation and levels of public expenditure.

It is argued that global political and economic convergence to a common liberal democratic regime marks 'The End of History' as a battle between capitalism and socialism (Fukuyama, 1992). Capitalism has won and the only question now is 'which variety?' The western options are the Anglo-American and the Rhineland models (Albert, 1993), and even those, it is argued, are being pushed towards economic convergence by powerful world forces. The major question for western capitalism concerns global competition (DofTandI, 1998) Western countries cannot compete in terms of costs with regions that are more able to provide cheap labour and make certain mass-produced goods at lower prices. Hence, wage competition will not guarantee prosperity. Instead, advanced production methods, research, information, and brand management are seen as alternative means to comparative advantage. The path to national prosperity therefore requires an investment in strategies which will enhance all of these. Consequences include a reduction in the availability of unskilled work and the need for a workforce that is educated and well-trained. Commercial and industrial competition is therefore at the centre of the policy picture and spending on redistribution and welfare services is a lower priority. Such shifts in policy are leading to the replacement of the traditional 'welfare state' with its 'high levels of benefit provision', 'high general taxation' and 'blunt-edged demand management' with the 'social investment state.' This values prevention and investment in the future over short-term welfare consumption. This transition has been described as a shift from the 'Keynesian Welfare State' to the 'Schumpeterian Workforce State' based on a productivist re-ordering of social policy (Jessop, 1994).

These changes can most easily be seen in approaches towards the unemployed. In the face of higher unemployment levels amongst working class unskilled and semi-skilled young men and amongst lone mothers, policy considerations in the 1990s, both in the UK and in the US, were increasingly dominated by discussions on 'workfare'. If welfare was provided on the basis that a person could not find work, workfare was introduced to top up wages and ease entry into a job. Job Seekers Allowance and Family Credits were introduced by the Conservative government and, because they blurred the line between employment and unemployment, can be seen as the most fundamentally new income maintenance schemes since 1945. In effect, they rewarded participation in work. In the UK, Labour's 'Welfare to Work' programmes involve clearer supervision of the lives of poor people who are expected to take action in return for benefits. They are in keeping with what Mead (1997) calls 'The New Paternalism'. New Paternalism is focussed on groups and individuals who are dependent on the state for income and support: for example, the working-aged poor, lone parents, those in the criminal justice system, people with poor health and those with low educational attainment. These are the people with whom social workers are most likely to come into contact.

Globalisation also has an impact on social workers in that attempts to reduce the costs of welfare have led to an increased reliance on the private and voluntary sector:

> ... the roles of the state and society in defining, protecting and promoting the public interest are being whittled away by a global campaign of privatisation and public sector commercialization driven by the needs of transnational business (Martin, 1993: cited in Cope, 1999, p. 53).

Attention will not be given here to this change as the topic is covered in chapter one and elsewhere in this volume. It is important to note, however, the part that globalisation is said to play, although globalisation is not all that is involved. According to Cope (1999), the shift away from the welfare state also involves the local preference for markets as a means of producing better and cheaper services.

The rise of managerialism within the public sector is also attributed, by some, to globalisation (see Hood, 1991). That is, the containment of spending on the welfare state can be achieved by managerial success in improving economy, effectiveness and efficiency. Dominelli and Hoogvelt (1996) trace globalisation, through managerialisation, to its impact on social work practice itself. However, as managerialisation has been covered in chapters two and four, mention is made here only to make some connections between recent developments.

Breaking European Boundaries

Europeanisation refers to the increased influence of the European Union (EU) on the nation states which belong to it. This influence can be direct, as in the commitment to common policies, or indirect as in the social consequences of economic convergence. States aspiring to belong might also be indirectly influenced: for example, they may pursue policies which enhance their chances of joining. Europeanisation, as a reaction to the threats associated with international competition, can be said to result (at least in part) from globalisation (Giddens, 1998 cited in Cope, 1999):

> Business, particularly big business, within the EU is highly dependent on free trade worldwide to buy imports and sell exports and consequently the EU has been at the forefront generally in pushing for the liberalisation of world trade, which has made states and societies more interconnected and thus more interdependent (Cope, 1999, p. 51).

Whilst globalisation is important, Cope (1999) argues that the foundations of the EU were laid after the Second World War when the six founding countries (West Germany, France, Italy, Belgium, the Netherlands and Luxembourg) committed themselves to a common market as a means of building their devastated economies. Political considerations were also at work as the move was an attempt to thwart a resurgence of Germany. Furthermore, America supported the development on the basis that a strong and coherent Europe could contain Soviet influence.

The UK joined the EU in 1973. Membership has always been contentious for the population of the UK who fear the loss of national sovereignty and take issue with many of the policies pursued. The situation is exacerbated by the fact that the nature of the EU can be incomprehensible to UK commentators because of its different public policy vocabulary. The EU's increasing concern with and influence on social matters is particularly contentious for the UK public. When the UK became a member state the basis for a social dimension had not been developed. The EU was about trade and economic integration rather than social harmonisation. The foundations of the social dimensions of the EU were put in place between 1984 and 1994 during the presidency of Jacques Delors. Delors promoted a 'social vision' for Europe which concentrated on unemployment, the protection of workers, equal opportunities in employment and training, and partnership between employers and employees. It was a highly corporatist approach, firmly within the European tradition of social democracy. For a time, it did seem that a common European policy framework for social welfare might well be created and there was talk of policy convergence.

Three key policy documents followed on from the Single European Act (1987) (which set out the firm intention of member states to create a unified free trade area within the Union) and raised the question of the subsequent harmonisation in social policy. The first document, the Treaty of the European Union (Maastricht, 1991) extended the aim to include greater economic convergence to underpin free trade, and supported more political co-operation to the same end. This was agreed by all member states. All member states but the UK signed the Social Chapter or Social Protocol which was the second document of the Delors era. It introduced the intention of the EU to ensure equal rights to social protection and access to employment, fair treatment for part-time workers who often had no employment protection, better working conditions, health and safety and access to training, equal treatment for men and women, the right to belong to a trade union and the entitlement of workers to receive information about the plans of larger companies. It also dealt with three issues of special relevance to social services. The first of these was a commitment to a decent standard of living for older people through adequate pension schemes, social care and health services. The second dealt with disabled people and their right to training, rehabilitation and integration into work. The third concerned the working conditions of people in social care, alongside other workers, in terms of minimum wage levels, working hours, shift patterns and entitlements. Given the diversity of views across the member states and the contentious issues contained within some of its provisions, the detailed implementation of the Social Chapter will take some time, if it happens at all.

The third key document during this period was the White Paper on European Social Policy (1994). This document both developed some provisions but also diluted some of the recommendations of the previous Green Paper. The differences between these two also marked an important transition from old style social democratic thinking about social welfare and social protection, to a new style of thinking about unemployment and the welfare state (see above). By this stage, the conditions necessary for European monetary union were of lively concern and governments were struggling to cope with the economic criteria for monetary convergence. High public spending was seen as a threat and there was some alarm at the implications of the rapidly ageing EU population, with its implied associated costs in pensions, financial entitlements, health care provision and the funding of long term care. It was clear at that point that the notion of a unified model for social welfare and social protection across Europe could not be achieved in the short-term and that the more pressing problems in the eyes of the European governments were cost containment and financial stability.

Despite this change of emphasis, the Maastricht Treaty, the Social Chapter and the White Paper were important milestones in the formal establishment of a social dimension in the policies of the EU. As a result of these developments the Commission has sponsored a significant programme of interventions around four themes - social insertion (into work and society), social cohesion, common social rights and common identity. Member states have been encouraged to adopt similar objectives for their social care systems, including adequate services for people in most need, the inclusion of disabled and disadvantaged people within mainstream society, the eradication of poverty (especially childhood poverty), and general improvements in living conditions of the worst off. They have also been encouraged to share best practice, and to co-operate with 'observatories' such as those on social exclusion, elderly citizens and family policies.

By the end of the Delors era the earlier optimism about the construction of a federal approach to welfare had been eroded. Nevertheless, concerns regarding the social implications of monetary union, changes in social relations and in family composition, and the demographic transformation of an ageing population have led to a new impetus for the development of European social policy. There is no intention to return to the old mechanisms of demand management, high welfare spending and high taxation. The new approach concentrates on the supply of labour, on education and training, and on policies to include people in work. Despite this focus on the labour market, the EU has also done much to place on the agenda questions concerning rights, equality and social exclusion.

The concept of social exclusion, and its related policies, has been embraced in the UK. Shortly after its election in 1997, the New Labour government introduced a Social Exclusion Unit to tackle specific problems such as teenage pregnancy and homelessness. Related initiatives have included New Deal for Communities, built around community decision making in very small areas, Sure Start, geographically targeted programmes for families with very small children and Health and Education Action Zones. However, the concept of social exclusion does not lie within the UK or US tradition of social analysis: its origins lie in France. It was the EU that took up and disseminated the concept, although in the early stages it was applied exclusively to the labour market. Social exclusion is related to the notion of social rights and responsibilities and the disadvantages created when these are not secured. Groups, such as the unemployed, can be defined by their exclusion whilst for others their identity can lead to their exclusion; as in the case of black people in a white society, for example. Hence, the concept is much broader than a concern for poverty. It offers the opportunity to go beyond snapshots of income/expenditure to a multi-dimensional analysis including other quality of life indicators (such as education, housing and health). It allows for a more dynamic analysis and changes the focus away from individuals and households towards 'the local community in its spatial dimension (Room, 1995).

Arguably, social projects involving local communities are properly the concern of social workers along with other professionals such as youth and community workers. Social Services Departments (SSDs) have always supported community groups, helped to lobby for resources, promoted benefit take-up campaigns and supported the creation of child care resources. According to Mosely (1998), social services staff have valuable knowledge about why and how social problems arise and the systems and circumstances that give rise to social exclusion. Hence, their knowledge and expertise should be called upon. Paradoxically, just at the time when community development is being promoted within policies dealing with social exclusion, SSDs across Europe have had to cut down this aspect of their work in the face of tight financial constraints and the requirement to focus on individuals deemed to be at risk.

Crossing and Building Boundaries: Economic Migration, Refugees and Asylum Seekers

People who have a different identity from the dominant group can be excluded. Identity is an all embracing term and can refer to physical and sensory ability but also skin colour, ethnicity, culture and religion. These characteristics are also mediated by gender, class and access to material resources. Recently arrived economic migrants, refugees and asylum seekers are groups of people who have crossed national boundaries and found themselves at the margins of a new society. They are also people with whom social workers often have contact. Services offered to such people vary as states within the EU have different approaches to people arriving from beyond their boundaries. Some offer citizenship easily but then limit welfare provision when there is an economic downturn (France for example). Other countries, like Germany, offer welfare provision more generously but restrict citizenship. The debate across Europe has been about diversity between groups, the terms of citizenship and the exclusion of some by their segregation in poor housing, poorly paid work or no work at all and accommodation in areas under greatest stress. Formal citizenship by itself may provide no solution to these problems which are about social and economic power and differential resources.

The conflicts during the 1990s in the Balkans have thrown into sharp relief the refugee question across the whole of Europe. Refugees are involuntary migrants who were reluctant to uproot themselves and who have moved in anticipation of violence or in response to it (Zolberg, 1989). They are protected within Europe by the UN Convention on the Status of Refugees and states are prohibited from expelling them to a country where they risk persecution. They are guaranteed a right to apply for asylum, but not to obtain it - that is the sole discretion of the state to which they have travelled. The involuntary character of migration is very evident in relation to Bosnia and Kosovo. However, others claiming that they are refugees (for example, those from the Baltic States, Roumania and Albania) have not been so been well received. Similarly, asylum seekers from Africa have not been well-regarded by the European authorities even when they have fled war zones. The idea of persecution is a contested variable and there exists a *de facto* hierarchy of more or less acceptable groups of refugees. In 1985 nine EU countries signed the Schengen Accord, by which they agreed to co-ordinate their policies on migration, asylum, border controls and visa requirements. This was the beginning of a process intended to protect Western Europe from instability elsewhere. Although not all EU countries belong to this Accord, it was a step towards the building of Fortress Europe. Hence, for citizens of the EU the boundaries between EU states may be crossed freely but citizenship may not be readily granted, and the boundaries around the EU have been made less permeable.

Global Social Work?

The influences described in the previous sections demonstrate that the global economy and developments in Europe are having an impact on social policy in the UK. The global movement of people creates new challenges around the question of exclusion - exclusion from Europe but also social exclusion within. Social services and social work are influenced both directly and indirectly by all the above. An important question arises from this fact: how far is social work itself breaking boundaries and becoming a universal phenomenon?

Social work as a profession evolved in North America and Europe (see chapter four) and has become well established in South America,

Africa and South East Asia. Japan has a long, if limited involvement with social work. China is increasingly interested, and many of the member states of the former Soviet Union are adopting social work as an integral part of the new social fabric of their countries (see chapter seven). Although social work was absent from most communist regimes, both Poland and the former Yugoslavia have long established social work traditions. Social work flourished in Czechoslovakia before 1939 and has been reborn there since 1990. Worldwide there are now thought to be nearly 1,800 schools of social work in over 100 countries. If this is taken as an indicator of social work activity then as a phenomenon it is almost universal around the globe.

Kahn and Kamerman (1978) argued that, as social and personal problems were universal, then so would be the provision of social services. Although it was recognised that cultures would highlight certain problems over others, and responses would vary, it was argued that cross-national evaluation and the sharing of experience would be beneficial. The work of Kahn and Kamerman is based on the optimistic belief that common human needs would generate broadly similar institutional responses. However, since the 1970s, there have been major threats to the development of a common (or at least similar) approach to social work. These have resulted from the recognition of difference and, paradoxically, the importance of the local context. More specifically these threats emerge from three sources: from service users, their carers and their advocates; from the body of experience outside of Western nations; and from within the heartland of the applied social sciences themselves. Social workers in the UK are quite familiar with movements such as the 'social disabilities' movement and forms of advocacy that have questioned the nature and relevance of social work expertise to empowerment (Croft and Beresford, 1990). In the Third World, the marked differences in local cultures and developments have undermined the claim that social work is based on universal values and principles. Western literature on social work has been exposed for relying on Eurocentric conceptions of family, community and individual identity (see Ahmed, 1993 and Graham, 1999). How relevant then are western ideas about social work to non-Western countries and to minority ethnic communities with external roots living in the west?

All these developments are reflected in social theory. Postmodernism has challenged enlightenment thinking: certainties concerning objective truth and progress have been undermined. Postmodernism has questioned the vision of universal social services, leading to the conclusion by some writers that advancement is not inevitable and there is no universal design for services (Carter, 1998). According to postmodern thought, society is made up of shifting coalitions and random patterns of contacts associated with multiple identities and discourses. Under these circumstances it is impossible to prescribe common models of social work and social work effectiveness. Social work is intrinsically different with different groups and interests, and the claim for commonality is itself a form of oppression. As a result, the emphasis on differences de-stablises the 'grand narratives' about social welfare and the welfare state which were prominent in the post-war period. Because the over-arching framework of social progress has disintegrated, governments are increasingly attempting to 'micro-manage' the small scale results of social interventions and thereby to manage some part of the larger chaos. The performance indicators given to Social Services Departments by the UK government are an example of this attempt.

Many of the trends associated with postmodernisation have been identified in earlier chapters. The paradoxical implication is that, despite globalisation and Europeanisation, current thinking (reflected in the literature on postmodernism) is frequently against the idea of universal social welfare and social work. However, not all theorists subscribe to this view. Doyal and Gough (1991) make a spirited defence of the importance of defining fundamental human needs. They argue that, once defined, common approaches can be found that will help people despite the wide variety of social circumstances facing public services. They argue that needs are preconditions for human action, and that physical health and personal autonomy are the basic prerequisites for any forms of life. Hence, Doyal and Gough confirm the foundational values and aims of social work. They recognise that humans are being harmed by social circumstances and that social change designed to minimize serious harm can still be regarded as progressive. Hence, whilst acknowledging the complexity of life and the problem of relativism in the social sciences, Doyal and Gough resist the idea that progress is impossible. They conclude that progress is best achieved in a regime which balances democratic and participatory arrangements, state intervention, voluntary activity and private enterprise. Many different organisational forms are consistent with their principles which are about desirable outcomes as well as acceptable methods. Hence, for Doyal and Gough universal principles of social welfare and social work can apply even if methods of delivery and specific practices vary across the globe.

Discussion and Conclusion

It is interesting that recent theoretical attention has been devoted to highlighting either global or local influences on social policy and social services. Some theorists have challenged the globalisation thesis on the grounds that its impact is mediated locally. For example, theorists such as Taylor-Gooby (1996) argue that nations respond differently to similar global influences. According to Wilding (1997), local demographics and preferred ideologies mediate the impact of global influences. Furthermore, argues Wilding, it is impossible to separate out, let alone measure, the significance of local influences from the global. Robertson suggests that it is more appropriate to think in terms of 'glocalisation' - 'the simultaneity and the interpretation of what is conventionally called the global and the local' (Robertson 1995, p. 30 cited in Cope, 1999, p. 47).

Whilst it might appear paradoxical that the global and the local have both been of recent theoretical interest, on closer examination there is a relationship between the two. Many of the features of postmodern welfare identified above relate to, or depend upon, globalisation. For example, reduced professional autonomy is, in part, a result of new managerialism and attempts to develop effective and economic welfare in the face of constrained budgets and international economic competition (see chapters two and four in this volume). Indeed, both globalisation and postmodernism belong to what has been described as the 'modernity thesis' (O'Brien and Penna, 1998). From this viewpoint, principles of the Enlightenment no longer apply, and current society is markedly different from that which has gone before.

Despite the importance of the local and the diverse experiences of individual countries, it is clear that recent trends are moving towards an increasing interdependence and interconnectedness between states. Whether this interconnectedness enhances or reduces a state's ability to form policy is also open to debate. Whilst note has been made of the argument that states have been 'hollowed out', others suggest that this is not the case: whilst there has been a re-configuration of powers, the state's role has not been reduced (see for example Panitch, 1994 and Weiss, 1998). According to Cope:

> Such reorganising or shifts as Europeanisation, privatisation and NPM [New Public Managerialism] may actually enhance the managing capacity of the state. British government arguably manages interdependence most effectively inside, rather than outside the EU by striking intergovernmental

bargains; it arguably exerts more influence over regulated privatised industries operating within a greater (though not great) competitive environment than if it owned them. And it arguably controls public services more tightly by introducing NPM reforms. Rather than these trends representing a displacement of state powers, they may represent a reconfiguration and even rejuvenation of those powers (Cope, 1999, p. 58).

Globalisation is said to have created or exacerbated certain problems, for example: AIDS, drug abuse, sex tourism, unemployment and migration (Wilding, 1997). Whilst it has not been possible to cover all of these issues, some attention has been given to the question of migration and the European response. Despite attempts to harmonise approaches within Europe, the example of migrants reveals the different responses of individual states. Similarly, attempts to harmonise approaches to welfare have had only limited success. The question of whether common solutions can ever be found has been raised along with debates concerning universal social services and social work. The only conclusion that can be drawn is that, in these modern times the most common feature of social work and social care is change, and that this applies beyond the boundaries of the UK to Europe and further afield.

References

Ahmed, A. (1993), *Living Islam*, BBC, London.
Albert, M. (1993), *Capitalism against Capitalism*, Whurr, London.
Carter, J. (1998), *Postmodernity and the Fragmentation of Welfare*, Routledge, London.
Cope, S. (1999), 'Globalisation, Europeanisation and Management of the British State' in S. Horton and D. Farnham (eds), *Public Management in Britain*, Macmillan, Basingstoke.
Croft, S. and Beresford, P. (1990), *From Paternalism to Participation. Involving People in Social Services*, Open Services/Joseph Rowntree Foundation, London.
DofTandI (Department of Trade and Industry) (1998), *Our Competitive Future: Building the Knowledge Driven Economy*, Stationary Office, London.
Dominelli, L. and Hoogvelt, A. (1996), 'Globalization and the Technocratization of Social Work', *Critical Social Policy*, vol. 16, pp. 45-62.
Doyal, L. and Gough, I. (1991), *A Theory of Human Need*, Macmillan, Basingstoke.
Fukuyama, F. (1992), *The End of History and the Last Man*, Penguin, Harmondsworth.
Giddens, A. (1998), *The Third Way*, Polity Press, Cambridge.
Graham, M.J. (1999), 'The African-Centred World View: Developing a Paradigm for Social Work', *British Journal of Social work*, vol. 29, no. 4, pp. 251-67.
Hirst, P. and Thompson, G. (1996), *Globalization in Question*, Polity Press, Cambridge.
Hood, C. (1991), 'A Public Management for All Seasons', *Public Administration*, vol. 69, no. 1, pp. 3-19.

Jessop, B. (1994), 'The Transition to Post-Fordism and the Schumpterian Workfare State' in R. Burrows and B. Loader (eds), *Towards a Post-Fordist Welfare State?*, Routledge, London.

Kahn, A. and Kamerman, S. (1978), *Social Services in International Perspective*, US Department of Health, Welfare and Education, Washington.

Martin, B. (1993), *In the Public Interest: Privatization and Public Sector Reform*, Zed Books, London.

McGrew, A. (1992), 'A Global Society?', in S. Hall, D. Held and T. McGrew (eds), *Modernity and its Future*, Cambridge Polity Press/Open University Press, Buckingham.

Mead, L.M. (1997), *The New Paternalism*, Brookings, Washington DC.

Mosely, J. (1998), '*A Developing Role*', Community Care, 26th February, pp. 6-7.

O'Brien, M. and Penna, S. (1998), *Theorising Welfare. Enlightenment and Modern Society*, Sage, London.

Panitch, L. (1994), 'Globalisation and the State', in R. Miliband and L. Panitch (eds), *Socialist Register 1994: Between Globalisation and Nationalism*, Merlin Press, London.

Robertson, R. (1995), 'Globalization: Time-Space and Homogeneity-Heterogeneity', in M. Featherstone, S. Lash and R. Robertson (eds), *Global Modernities*, Sage, London.

Room, G. (ed.) (1995), 'Poverty and Social Exclusion: The New European Agenda for Policy and Research', in *Beyond the Threshold: The Measurement of Analysis of Social Exclusion*, Policy Press, Bristol.

Taylor-Gooby, P. (1996), ''Eurosclerosis' in European Welfare States: Regime Theory and the Dynamics of Change', *Policy and Politics*, vol. 24, no. 2, pp. 109-24.

Weiss, L. (1998), *The Myth of the Powerless State*, Polity Press, Cambridge.

Wilding, P. (1997), 'Globalization, Regionalism and Social Policy', *Social Policy and Administration*, vol. 31, no. 4, pp. 410-28.

Zolberg, A.R. (1989), *Refugees*, Refugee Council, London.

7 Managing the Development of Social Work in Russia

VLADIMIR KOLKOV, BORIS SHAPIRO AND ALEXANDER SOLOVYOV

Introduction

Social work in Russia is a relatively new phenomenon. It was officially recognised only seven years ago. Before that time the term itself was not in use, although elements of the activity were incorporated into a vast network of welfare services. This network consisted of health, education, housing, leisure, employment and retirement. All services were run by the state. Since 1991 social work has been developing as an autonomous profession. In so doing it has emulated models known in the West and striven to assert itself in an environment that has not always been favourable to its growth.

The political and economic changes in Russia over recent years have led to an increase in social problems. Life is difficult for the majority of the population, but particularly so for vulnerable groups. The development of social work is a response to new challenges: it is a means of supporting those less fit for life's struggle and a device for promoting social integration. For social work to be successful in these goals it must first become established as a profession. In its formative stage, social work is in pursuit of its identity and public recognition. It is the primary goal of this chapter to draw attention to the developments that are taking place and to describe the context in which social work is attempting to shape itself.

Setting the Scene: Russia Before 1991

It is not easy to give an impartial assessment of the effect of the seven decades of communism on Russian society. Much depends on the frame of reference that is employed. There were indisputable achievements in the fields of education, health, science, technology and the arts. However, these achievements were not necessarily the direct result of the economic and political system. Many of them reflected the inevitable march of global civilisation in which Russians have always actively participated. Indeed, development itself was often one-sided, with seeds of potential conflicts germinating under the seemingly tranquil surface. For example, social stability was achieved through the suppression of civil liberties and a crackdown on all forms of political dissent. Full employment did not lead to genuine prosperity and only disguised serious economic problems. The quality of housing and medical services was poor by Western standards and disadvantaged people were not given the opportunity to integrate into mainstream society (Ramon, 1997).

At the same time, official propaganda proclaimed that by equitably distributing public wealth, socialism as a political system was capable of solving all basic human difficulties. Persistent social problems, like alcohol abuse, were played down and declared 'remnants of capitalism'. Such ideological tenets oriented social services towards improving material wellbeing of the people by containing 'social ills' and by providing material assistance to the most disadvantaged groups of the population. Social policy concentrated on building occupational welfare and safety nets for those unable to work, though the very term 'social policy' was not in use: policies were subsumed under the umbrella notion of the 'Party line'.

The term 'social work' was non-existent. The broad term 'social sphere' covered housing, health services and education, including 'special education' for children with disabilities and behaviour problems. The functions were divided between several state departments: the Ministry of Internal Affairs, the Education and Health Ministries, and the Ministry of Social Welfare. Unfortunately, there was little co-ordination between these different departments. Staff were recruited to each separate department and their training was limited to the rudiments of administration and accounting. The whole system functioned as a narrowly compartmentalised and bureaucratically organised network of state provision and social control. The system was paternalistic in nature with service users having practically no say in its running. The strong control function is illustrated by the fact that child protection was placed within the police and largely reduced to crime prevention. However, some elements of social work existed as part of an effective system of social security. This system was organised around the place of work with trade unions as major distributors of social benefits. Hence, the citizens of the USSR were dependent on their work for more than their salaries. Through their workplace they had access to housing, organised family holidays, and child care facilities. The Communist Party, especially its youth branches, was also actively involved in various forms of informal education which aimed to keep citizens abreast of official perspectives. In short, the system of social security in Russia consisted of three basic elements: provision for those unable to work; protection for those facing temporary hardship; and support for those incapable of managing life independently. The political and economic changes that took place in Russia in the late 1980s and the early 1990s made the system largely obsolete and called for new approaches to social welfare.

Recent Developments: Russia Since 1991

The demise of communism, the end of cold war, the break-down of the Soviet Union, the formation of democratic institutions and system of government – such were the major political developments during the last decade. In the economic sphere it was a time of transition from tight state control and central planning to a liberal system based on market principles. Russia has been progressively integrated into the world economy. However, the transition has been far from smooth and consequences have been painful for the Russian people. The freeing of consumer prices as a first step towards market reforms resulted in spiralling inflation with the inevitable loss of savings and a considerable drop in the living standard for the majority of the population.

The crisis in the Russian economy has been brought about by several factors: the disruption of traditional economic links within the former Soviet Union and East European Block, the enormous cost of dismantling the huge military machine; the inundation of the country with relatively cheap imported goods and the inability of many home producers to successfully compete internationally; and finally, the drop in oil prices (with oil constituting the main Russian export). Despite being heavily supported by the international financial institutions, the economy has not yet produced signs of stable recovery. Industrial output is in decline. The programme of privatisation has been largely unable to turn the economic tide. Tax evasion is endemic and creates severe budgetary problems. Both external and internal debts weigh heavily on the national economy. The average national income is very low, particularly for those employed in the public sector. As a result, many people live below the poverty line. Delays in payments of salaries, pensions and social benefits add to the hardships. The economic crisis breeds widespread discontent and threatens to undermine civil order.

At the very start of the 1990s (just before the breakdown of the Soviet Union) scarcity of foodstuffs and basic consumer goods constituted the most serious economic and social problem in the county. The situation was caused by a change in the economic policy – a shift from strict state control over the production and distribution of goods towards more autonomous individual enterprises. The immediate effect was twofold. Firstly, liberated from tough central regulation and not constrained by market forces, enterprises gained a free hand to increase their workers' salaries without a parallel increase in productivity. The result was too much money in circulation and too few goods to meet the demand. The shops were soon empty and long queues for food (bread, milk, butter, and meat) became a constant feature of everyday life. To cope with the situation rationing for basic foodstuffs was introduced. Special coupons were issued for staple food, tobacco and alcohol. Secondly, under communism enterprises were compelled to produce cheap consumer goods. When the pressure was removed, they switched to producing expensive goods targeted at more prosperous sections of the population. This, in turn, stimulated inflation and further exacerbated the situation both for the ordinary consumer and the national economy as a whole. The quality of consumer goods produced in the country remained low since obsolete technologies and equipment were used to manufacture them. Customers were quite aware of the fact and clearly preferred imported goods. As a result, new problems confronted home producers when the trade barriers formerly protecting them were removed.

The political course adopted by the new Russian administration after the collapse of the Soviet Union at the end of 1991 combined sweeping market reforms with openness towards the outside world. The free press was active in criticising the old economic and political system. At the same time, it bombarded the audience with information about high living standards in the world's most developed countries. The radical transition to a free market involving 'shock therapy' was advocated as the best solution to Russia's many problems. The idea of a smooth transition of a type favoured, for example, by China had been discarded. As noted above, the consequences of this approach have been painful.

With the end of The Cold War the 'iron curtain' separating the Soviet bloc countries from the rest of the world gradually disappeared. Eventually this allowed imported goods to reach the Russian market and the balance between supply and demand was restored. On the surface it looked like a solution to the most pressing problem of total scarcity and the champions of the market economy hailed it as the advent of the long awaited 'consumer paradise'. In fact, the situation was far from satisfactory. Serious structural problems were accumulating. The weak Russian rouble was largely supplanted by the American dollar which became a parallel currency. Home producers were mostly unable to compete with their foreign rivals. The national economy fell into a deep crisis with all major indicators decreasing sharply. This in turn caused a glaring budget deficit with all the dire consequences for the social programmes. The government tried to remedy the situation by borrowing heavily from abroad. The growing external debt, however, has created an additional pressure on the weak national economy. The ultimate economic stabilisation predicted by the reformers has not yet materialised. Moreover, a new economic crisis broke out in August 1998 further straining the precarious political situation in the country and demonstrating that the period of transition started in the mid-1980s is far from over.

The political, economic and social situation in Russia changed fundamentally in the late 1980s with the demise of communism. Freedom of the press was introduced and the mass media started exploring and revealing the true scope of social problems facing the country. By contrast with the previous rosy picture, the real situation looked gloomy. This in turn produced a psychological shock amongst the general population. It is worth keeping in mind that in former times many types of official statistics were treated as classified information thus being inaccessible to public scrutiny. When data on crime and substance misuse were finally disclosed they looked alarming. Furthermore, the new approach to presenting social issues to the public had an impact. Freed from ideological control from above, the mass media dwelt on the unhappier sides of life. Front pages of the national newspapers may serve as a clear indication of the sea change. In former times they invariably displayed photos of well-fed and happy-looking people at work or at leisure. More recently, they have become swamped by images of misery and squalor. Social optimism actively promoted by the former regime has given way to widespread public despair.

The Current Situation and Its Causes

To give a balanced assessment of the current situation and the changes that have taken place is again not an easy task. Even official figures can be misleading in that they do not take account of the many covert factors at play. It is known that Russian citizens spend twice as much as they (officially) earn. This means that people conceal their real incomes to avoid paying taxes. At the same time, the wages of state employees are very low in comparison with consumer prices. Today, the minimal wage in Russia is only 7 per cent of the average wage compared to 20 per cent in most developed countries. The subsistence level is 75 per cent of the average wage. Therefore, the official minimal wage is far below the present subsistence level and there are now about 250 types of various statutory benefits (Korostikova, 1999).

The switch to a market economy produced sharp divisions within Russian society. A new class of the rich appeared: mostly fairly young people running their own private companies. In many cases the line between legitimate business and illegal activities became blurred and the Mafia soon asserted itself as a powerful element in the Russian economy. The 'shadow' economy comprises 40 per cent of the national economy with wages paid at twice the rate of the official average. The gap between the rich and the poor widened, producing more social tension. Recent estimates are that today, 65 per cent of national assets belong to only 1.5 per cent of Russian citizens. The average income of the well-to-do (the upper 10 per cent of the scale) compared to that of the poorly provided (the lower 10 per cent) is 14 times higher (Zaslavskaya, 1998). The income differential between the highest and the lowest wages in Russia is now 26 times (48 times in Moscow). The salaries of senior managers are on average 26 times higher than of rank-and-file workers, while ten years ago the ratio was 4:1. Clearly, recent developments have increased financial hardship for most Russian people and previous safety nets have proved inadequate. In addition, the changed social and political context has led to social ills which are new to Russia. One new problem is unemployment. Estimates made by the Ministry of Labour and Social Development suggest that 8.5 million (11.5 per cent of all employable people) are currently out of work. However, only 1,750,000 people (one in five) are officially registered as unemployed. Thus, hidden unemployment is in the region of 7-8 million (officially 4-5 million). The regional distribution of unemployment is as follows: 1 per cent in Moscow and 7-8 per cent in the most severally hit areas of the country. These areas were traditionally heavily dependent on the military, textile and mining industries for employment. Young people between 16 and 29 make up a sizeable proportion of the unemployed (*The Independent Gazette* – Political Economy, 1998).

As indicated above, the reduction in the Russian armed forces has contributed to Russia's social problems. During the period of 1994–98 half a million officers were demobilised. The huge task of resettling all these people and readjusting them to civil life has not been fully tackled even with the money provided by Germany specially for the purpose. By now, less than one-tenth of these people have managed to undergo retraining to acquire a new profession. Almost half of them have not yet been provided with permanent accommodation. No wonder that thousands of former servicemen in their desperate search for income end up joining the army of criminals (*Arguments and Facts Weekly*, 1998a).

Unemployment is not the only social problem currently troubling Russia. The proportion of neglected children has risen sharply and the number of so-called 'street children' is estimated to be close to a million. This problem of children living on the streets has been described as comparable to the aftermath of the two major wars of this century. The police report that over recent times as many as 100,000 babies have been abandoned by their parents. These children are cared for in institutions. There are several hundred known cases of parents selling their children for the average sum of 2,000-5,000 dollars (*Arguments and Facts Weekly*, 1998b). The crime rate amongst young people is also very high. The figures released by the police show that young offenders are responsible for approximately 100,000 criminal acts annually. There has been a sharp rise in the number of girls involved in this type of activity. In the past five years, there has been a 34.4 per cent increase of girls under the age of 14 years committing offences (*Arguments and Facts Weekly*, 1997). Young people are also becoming involved in drug abuse – a problem that was hardly known in Russia prior to the collapse of communism.

The unfavourable social situation is also reflected in the reduced life expectancy and low birth rate. Consequently, the population of Russia is decreasing by one million each year. The projections suggest that if the trend continues the population of the country will halve by the year 2060 (*The Russian Gazette*, 1997). The suicide rate has also risen sharply during the past decade. Lately, it has reached the level of over 60,000 per annum. This is more than the number of people (about 45,000) murdered every year. Compared to European figures, the suicide rate in Russia is 2.5 times higher for men and 1.5 higher for women (*Arguments and Facts Weekly*, 1998c).

The political opposition has contributed to the psychological distress of the nation by drawing attention to, and often exaggerating, the extent of suffering and social injustice. However, the vast majority of Russians were mentally unprepared for the sweeping changes. For decades they had been conditioned to rely on the state for the satisfaction of their basic needs. 'Certainty about tomorrow' had always been presented by Soviet propaganda as the greatest achievement of socialism. This helps to explain why the recent dramatic changes have produced feelings of anxiety and depression. Senior citizens, with their savings eroded by inflation and their pensions made inadequate, were amongst those hardest hit by the 'shock therapy'. Not surprisingly, many of them felt nostalgic for the former times and joined the ranks of the political opposition. It has become clear that at this time of transition, people need psychological support no less than the purely material.

The Emerging Institute of Social Work

On the positive side, it must be acknowledged that the hard times stimulated new developments in the way the social services were run. Ultimately social work was recognised as a vital component of a civilised society. New agencies, both statutory and non-governmental, sprang into being. The voluntary sector was revived through such new tasks as the distribution of the incoming Western aid and through direct contacts with volunteers coming from abroad to help Russians in their plight. More people were drawn into the activity. The need for qualified personnel was strongly felt at all levels of the service. Managerial skills acquired particular importance in the transitional period from tightly state-controlled economy to free market. To meet the demand, special training programmes were launched, often with the assistance of colleagues from abroad. Currently the total number of people employed in various social services across the country is estimated at over 120,000, though the majority of them have not yet undertaken formal training.

Social work education was introduced to universities in 1991 and has since expanded rapidly. Today there are more than 100 schools of social work in Russia. Two professional organisations have been formed: the Association of Social Pedagogues and Social Workers, and the Association of Social Services. Professional publications have begun to appear and international contacts have intensified considerably. This, in turn, has stimulated the reappraisal of many existing practices. All these are clear indications that social work in Russia is successfully developing as a profession (Solovyov, 1996; 1998).

At the beginning of the transitional period, social pedagogy was a convenient model upon which to build Russian social work. In contrast to mainstream teachers who are responsible for the formal instruction of pupils, social pedagogues have been responsible for extramural activities which have broader educational objectives: for example, encouraging young people to comply with accepted social norms and helping those with behavioural disorders. A related branch of pedagogical science called 'defectology' was engaged in educating children with special needs. Russia could boast of some impressive achievements in this area. For example, a highly successful programme of remedial training for children suffering from a combination of blindness and deafness was developed by the Research Institute of Defectology and implemented in a specialised boarding school near Moscow. Some of these pupils went on to study at university.

The term 'social pedagogue' was imported from Germany and Sweden, but the discipline and practice has been well developed in Russia for some time. During the Soviet era the area was highly politicised and known under the name of 'communist education'. Nevertheless, certain practical accomplishments here clearly overcome the narrow ideological confines imposed by the orthodox doctrine. For example, the spectacular results achieved by Makarenko in the early 1920s in re-educating former street children and bringing them into mainstream life are well publicised. His approach incorporated principles of respect for the person, trust and collective activity. In the 1970s and 1980s participatory school education was advocated by some prominent pedagogues as an alternative to the more traditional authoritarian and paternalistic style of teaching. Thus, the existing practice of special education for people with disabilities coupled with the experience in re-socialising 'problem teenagers' provided a foundation for the development of what in the West was traditionally known as 'social work'. As the young generation was the prime target of the efforts, the term 'social pedagogy' seemed quite appropriate. But for the more comprehensive approach to helping the aged, the sick and other specific groups it appears to be too narrow and the more inclusive term 'social work' is now generally accepted as preferable.

The new Constitution of the Russian Federation aims to create a welfare state that has a broad network of social services for families and various vulnerable groups. However, the present circumstances appear to be highly unfavourable for its implementation. The existing structure of social security built largely under the previous regime proves far from adequate in the current economic and social conditions. The state agencies comprising it are not dynamic enough to respond to new developments and changing needs. On the other hand, various political parties, religious organizations, voluntary associations and charitable foundations more directly representing the interests of diverse social groups are too weak to effect an alternative social policy. The civil society in Russia is just emerging and social rights have not yet been incorporated into the legal framework. In practice, social policy is generally reduced to social protection understood as the guaranteed basic material wellbeing for everyone. More subtle individual needs are virtually ignored (Shapiro, 1996).

Welfare provision in Russia is regulated at three levels: federal, regional, and local. The federal government and its branches are involved in forming and sustaining statutory mechanisms aimed at meeting basic needs of the population at large. One function is establishing scales for pensions, subsidies and other benefits so as to guarantee the subsistence level for the majority of those unable to provide for themselves. In December 1995 a federal law defining the principles of welfare provisions was adopted and this currently serves as a legal framework for all relevant efforts. At the regional level, Russia is now divided into 89 large territorial units with two major cities – Moscow and St. Petersburg – accorded this status. Each unit has its own budget and its own special bodies responsible for the allocation of the available resources. Co-ordination between various programmes (educational, medical, social) is implemented predominantly at this level. Territorial bodies have powers to prioritise the tasks and single out special target groups as subjects for additional entitlements. At the local (municipal) level, a network of social services is formed according to the needs of the population and the available resources. The needy and the vulnerable constitute the bulk of the clients. The major forms of welfare provision are: material support, home help, residential care, day care centres, temporary shelters, counselling and rehabilitation. According to the current law, statutory agencies can offer a range of paid services, but in practice, they are financed almost entirely from public funds. Latterly there is much talk about the need to promote consumer choice through introducing market principles into the field and turning service users into direct purchasers of services. However, at this point the idea seems too radical since its adoption entails an overhaul of the whole system.

Russian social policy has always been paternalistic in its main orientation. It means that the state directly provides benefits and services. Moreover, it is the state, represented by its various official bodies, that defines the needs of citizens. Service users are seen as passive recipients of benefits distributed according to strict prescriptions by 'experts'. The shift towards a market economy calls for a more equitable relationship between service users and service providers, with the former playing a more active part in shaping the services and assessing their effectiveness. However, the inertia of the existing system and the accepted ways of thinking make re-orientation rather slow. For a number of historical reasons, social work in Russia tends to accept the so-called 'medical model' as its basic professional ideology. There is a close fit between this approach to choosing the appropriate methods of social work and the paternalistic principle of service delivery in general. Both tend to place the important decisions about the fate of the clients entirely into the hands of professionals who are supposed to act on behalf of society. Service users are regarded as lacking in some essential qualities, as possessing a 'defect', as deviating from the accepted 'norm'. Therefore, the aim of professional intervention is to correct the 'defect', to bring them back to the mainstream of society. Professionals in their capacity as experts, define the 'problems' and the desirable ways of solving them. As agents of the society (the state) they feel themselves entitled to interfere into the lives of their clients and to impose their will couched in the form of expert judgements. The function of control is either overtly paramount or disguised as care.

Another problem in the development of social work involves the attitudes which prevail within Russian society. Compared to much of the Western world there is a lack of sympathy towards feminist perspectives and ethnic minorities. Liberal traditions have not been strong in Russia. The monarchy in the nineteenth century and the communist regime in the twentieth century were highly autocratic and brutally suppressive of any dissent. Liberal traditions have never been strong in Russia. Civil society is just beginning to take root and plurality of opinion and lifestyles is not celebrated by the majority of the population. Discrimination in the form of sexism, ageism, and disablism are quite common. Disabled persons are treated with commiseration but without much respect for their human rights. They suffer not only from their disability as such, but also from the stigma attached to it. All this creates an environment less favourable for social work than in the West.

The historical links of present day social work in Russia with what was termed 'ideological work' under communism also have certain repercussions in the current professional culture. One of them is unwillingness on the part of some social work managers and educators, including the high ranking, to draw on the relevant Western experience in the field. In fact, the insistence on 'the distinct Russian way' represents a thinly covered hankering to restore the discarded totalitarian practices of tackling social problems. Here again we have a basic ideological division in Russian society with one ('progressive') part looking to the West for proven recipes and another ('conservative') resenting any 'foreign inference'. As has been already noted, current social work practice in Russia is basically reduced to the collection and primary analysis of data on people in need and to the distribution of material benefits (money, food, clothing, medicines etc.). This means that more complex psychosocial needs of the clients are often neglected, their coping ability is not optimised and the potential of bringing them back to independent living is not used to the full. Therefore, the overall effectiveness of social work intervention, which is reactive rather than proactive, remains relatively low with root causes of the problems not addressed (Shapiro, 1996).

Compared to its Western counterparts, social work in Russia reveals other weaknesses. For example, specialised areas of practice are divided between several government bodies: the Ministry of Education is responsible for children with learning difficulties; the Ministry of Internal Affairs, for juvenile delinquents and offenders; the Labour and Employment Committee, for the unemployed; the Ministry of Health Care, for the sick, the disabled and people with alcohol and drug related problems; the Ministry for Crisis Situations cares for the victims of natural and industrial disasters as well as for refugees; the Ministry of Labour and Social Development is engaged in welfare provisions for various categories of vulnerable people. Although the activities of these ministries often overlap, insufficient co-ordination between them leads to a dissipation of effort and prevents a truly holistic (multidisciplinary) approach to tackling the issues.

Certain areas of specialised practice (e.g. child abuse, domestic violence, loss and bereavement) are clearly undeveloped in Russia. On the societal level these issues are largely taboo. On the practical level group social work (including self-help groups) is virtually non-existent. Here again, contacts with colleagues from abroad are important for Russian social workers, for they stimulate reflection on the existing practice and provide a wealth of new ideas on how it could be improved. Nevertheless, the recent growth in the social services is quite impressive. Table 7.1 reflects the rapid growth in the number of new social services directed mostly at child protection and rehabilitation. The growth in the number of more traditional agencies is not so dramatic. Partly it can be explained by the fact that they were largely in place when the transformation started. Partly it reflects the new priorities in the provision of services. The public sector remains the main provider of social services though there is a trend towards greater diversification of service providers. Both voluntary and commercial organisations are beginning to play a part in this field, though overall their contribution remains quite modest. They are not yet fully developed and integrated into a comprehensive network. The actual demand for social services is much greater than existing agencies (both statutory and independent) can meet.

Table 7.1 Growth in social work provision

Social work institutions	1994	1995	1996	1997	1998
Centres of social assistance to children and families	36	92	169	190	259
Social shelters for children and teenagers	22	173	311	390	388
Centres of social rehabilitation for juvenile delinquents	7	61	116	159	206
Centres of social rehabilitation for children with disabilities	33	94	138	151	152
Psychological and educational centres	3	88	100	123	151
Gerontology centres	-	5	15	25	40
Telephone hotlines (psychological crisis help)	5	78	80	93	148
Night shelters	17	35	80	100	120
Day centres	180	320	500	750	850
Social services centres	321	565	800	1,000	1,200
Emergency social units	635	1,050	1,500	1,600	1,700
Community social services	7,833	8,829	10,220	11,670	12,110

Source: Russian Ministry of Labour and Social Development (1998)

The development of social work in Russia is seriously hampered by negative factors located outside the profession itself. Much remains to be done in order to achieve its wide recognition as a vital component of a civilised society. Social workers must be adequately paid and they must have extensive knowledge, particular personal qualities and commitment. The tasks involved are stressful and even dangerous at times. Hence, the profession must have the support of its society. Unfortunately, this is not the case in Russia today. The majority of social workers in the country are employed in state-run agencies and salaries for state employees are extremely low compared to those in the commercial sector. Often they are barely sufficient to guarantee the minimally acceptable standard of living.

In these circumstances social services are unable to attract people with appropriate credentials. The best graduates are drawn into the commercial sector. The problems, however, are not only material in character. Social work remains a low-prestige occupation. Even in the West where the profession has been established for some time its status is not high. In Russia, most people are unaware of its existence. Even if they are aware of it, they associate it only with material provision for the poor. Most officials at central and local levels grossly underestimate its true potential. Areas such as psychosocial work and community organization are in their infancy. The ideas of advocacy, empowerment and self-help activism have only recently been introduced. Hence, raising public awareness of the potential of social work is important if the profession is to survive. Social work education, too, must become education in the broadest sense of the word: a force for improving the human condition at large.

The rapid expansion of social work education attests the high demand for qualified practitioners and bodes well for the successful development of the profession as it gradually asserts itself and gains prestige. However, the rapid growth creates another set of problems; the quality of training being one of them. Educators themselves are new to the profession, coming from various related disciplines: philosophy, sociology, psychology, history etc. Many have never had direct experience of working with vulnerable people. They draw on the body of theoretical knowledge, but they lack the relevant background to be able to transfer practical experience (Ramon, 1997).

The Potential for Improvement

Social work practitioners in Russia turn increasingly to the West to use collective experience for guiding principles and professional standards. Here a certain contradiction is bound to arise. On the one hand, social work takes place in a particular historical context and therefore must accommodate itself to the prevailing practices and societal norms. On the other, social work as an active force is always oriented towards change and strives to promote a better social order. In this role it assumes a critical stance towards the existing state of affairs, questions the ingrained attitudes underlying various forms of discrimination and injustice. Hence, the inevitable clash between 'realism' and 'idealism', between what is and what should be. A positive move forwards is to start to shape a comprehensive social policy aimed at creating a welfare state with two coordinated goals in view. Firstly, there must be resources and an infrastructure to provide personalised support for those who are currently experiencing serious problems in their lives. Secondly, social work must be proactive in directing efforts at addressing the causes of social problems. New social policy calls for new modes of service delivery with the emphasis on more direct and personalised provision. The system must be more sensitive to the needs of various user groups through their closer involvement in service planning and evaluation. Networking between different service providers is another important direction of development. The aim here is to provide service packages tailored to the particular client's needs. The current system is not comprehensive. It is patchy and fragmented with many vital elements missing. The shift from highly centralised and impersonal structure of social services towards a system more responsive to community need will help to bring it more in tune with the basic values of social work as they are defined by the international professional community. A mixed arrangement with wider participation of voluntary and private concerns appears to be more appropriate for achieving a positive change. The development of alternative forms of service delivery alongside statutory agencies is one way of addressing the challenge posed by the present-day situation in Russia.

We believe that at this point a key issue for social policy and social work in Russia is to formulate an overarching philosophy guiding the choice of priorities and of those approaches to practice which are best suited to address them. Despite some resistance, the Western experience can assist here. Russia today is undergoing a process of transition to a Western-style democracy. Thus, both the issues these societies have to face in their day-to-day functioning and the solutions they apply are of high relevance to those following suit. As noted above, the so-called 'medical model' remains the dominant approach to social work in Russia. In the West this has been contested and the 'participation model' has become popular. For example, in terms of disability, the concepts of 'rehabilitation', 'normalisation', 'enabling', 'empowerment', 'reintegration into the community', and 'social valorisation' have become important and are more in tune with the humanistic values espoused by the social work profession. Instead of speaking about 'intervention', 'correction' and 'treatment', social workers now speak of facilitation and advocacy. They urge their clients to take positive steps towards independent living and self-directed and self-help groups. To promote such an approach to disability, social work professionals must challenge the traditional practices and stereotypes that are deeply entrenched in the mind of the Russian public.

Participative approaches are difficult to introduce in Russia. Throughout its history the country has been exposed to various types of authoritarian regimes with democracy struggling to maintain a firm basis in Russian society. Social services were traditionally run on prescribed state lines – as large state bureaucracies. Their staff perceived themselves first and foremost as public servants and agents of social control. Service users also tended to see them in that light. The power differential was high with clients expected to simply follow the directions of officials. This was reinforced by a society which looked to the state for protection and support. Against this background, ideas of civil rights (including social rights) and individual choice, are slow to gain wide acceptance. This makes the task of engaging service users in critical decisions difficult and challenging.

Conclusion

The strategic aim of social work is to improve the quality of life for the population in general and for the most vulnerable groups in particular. To achieve this, merely raising the number of service providers is not enough. It is necessary to implement fundamental changes in the way social services are organised and run. Material aid should be supplemented by psychosocial support. Personalised services of the latter type should become the key element of the system. It is necessary to co-ordinate the activities of various service providers and to expand this network to cover all parts of the country. Such an expansion creates a heightened demand for qualified personnel. The task of developing and improving the educational system becomes a major one for the profession at the moment. Given the lack of qualified educators and supervisors, a scarcity of textbooks, as well as the absence of accepted standards of professional competence, the task presents a great challenge to everyone concerned. All of this is within the context of great social upheaval. Social problems have increased and the social and material circumstances of most of the population, contrary to expectations, are in decline. There is political dissent as to the best way forward and some hanker after the certainties of the old regime. Nevertheless, a high degree of optimism continues to prevail and there is hope that with continued struggle, the effort invested so far will come to positive fruition.

References

Arguments and Facts Weekly (1997), no. 40, p. 11.
Arguments and Facts Weekly (1998a), no. 30, p. 10.
Arguments and Facts Weekly (1998b), no. 21, p. 11.
Arguments and Facts Weekly (1998c), no. 23, p. 14.
Korostikova, T. (1999), 'Wages Enough for a Decent Living', *Arguments and Facts Weekly*, no. 25, p. 8.
Ramon, S. (1997), 'The Development of Social Work and Social Work Education in Post-communist Russia', in B. Lesnik (ed.), *Change in Social Work*, Ashgate, Aldershot.
Russian Ministry of Labour and Social Development (1998), *The Bulletin of the Department on Family, Women and Children's Affairs*, no. 2.
Shapiro, B. (1996), 'Social Work Education: British Experience and Russian Reality', in S. Ramon and D. Kirton (eds), *What Future for Social Work Education?*, ATSWE Publications, Sheffield.
Solovyov, A. (1996), 'Social Work in Russia', in S. Ramon and D. Kirton (eds), *What Future for Social Work Education?*, ATSWE Publications, Sheffield.
Solovyov, A (1998), 'Introducing New Professions: The Case of Russian Social Work', in S. Ramon (ed.), *The Interface Between Social Work and Social Policy*, Venture Press, Birmingham.
The Independent Gazette, Political Economy (1998), no. 18, November.
The Russian Gazette (1997), 23 May.
Zaslavskaya, T. (1998), 'Social Stratification and Differentiation of Incomes in Russia', in S. Ramon (ed.), *The Interface Between Social Work and Social Policy*, Venture Press, Birmingham.

8 Social Work Management in Finland

MIKKO MÄNTYSAARI

Introduction

The aim of this chapter is to describe the current situation in Finnish social work management. How did social work develop in Finland? How did foreign influences affect the development of social work management? What are the current central management ideologies?

Firstly, some comments on the central concepts of this analysis are outlined. The concept 'social work management' is not yet widely used in Finland. Social work in public sector organisations is seen as a part of social and welfare administration. Social work is outlined by statute as one of the social services which, in Finland, also include a variety of social care services, for example, care for the elderly and for handicapped people, and day care for children. Social work in municipal social welfare offices is often combined with social assistance: much of Finnish social work involves dealing with the economic problems of clients, and a large part of social workers' time is spent on assessment of clients' needs and decision-making on social assistance cases. Because of this general administration framework, it is somewhat difficult to speak about social work administration as a separate entity. Social work management is part of a larger concept, namely social welfare management, or social administration.

The following discussion starts by presenting the formal structure of social welfare administration in Finland, together with data on the profile of social workers. A short review of the history of Finnish social welfare is then presented, concluding with an examination of management ideologies.

Historical Background of Social Welfare

Some historical context is necessary to understand social work and social administration in Finland. The peculiarities of Finnish society and its culture have strongly influenced the development of social administration. Finnish culture is a mixture of Western traditions - mainly coming from Sweden and Germany - and Eastern influences, emanating from Russia. Finland was a Swedish province from 1150 until 1809, when it was conquered by the Russians and became an autonomous Grand Duchy of the Russian Empire. During this time the Finns had the right to maintain existing Swedish laws and were granted extensive autonomy in internal affairs (Satka, 1995). Czarist Rule ended in 1917 when Finland declared itself an independent republic.

The development of Finnish social welfare administration had three major phases. The first period was the birth of modern poor relief, which coincided with the birth of the Finnish national ideology in the second half of the last century. The second phase started after 1918, when Finland became an independent republic. The third phase began in the years after the Second World War (Satka, 1995).

In common with developments in other countries, the ancestor of modern social work practices can be found in poor relief, which has a very long history, starting as far back as the eleventh century (Rauhala, 1996). According to Swedish law, poor relief was the responsibility of church parishes until 1865. Only in the few, and relatively small, cities was poor relief organised by local government. The increasing number of beggars and orphans drew more attention from the upper classes and so the Senate passed the first Poor Law (1852). This law was more or less copied from the Swedish Poor Law (Satka, 1995). Finnish poor relief workers were influenced by practices from Scandinavia, Germany and, to lesser degree, from England. Russian rule did not effect poor relief administration, but on a more general level, the Czarist administrative culture did influence Finnish administrative systems and processes.

The second period in the development of social welfare administration began at the time of Finnish independence (1917) and the aftermath of the Finnish civil war in 1918. Deep social divisions in rural areas between land-owners and farmers without their own land, and the severe food shortage in industrial areas, lead to social unrest. The October revolution in Russia made Finnish independence possible. However, social divisions in Finland were not resolved. The civil war, with many injured and orphans especially on the vanquished 'Red' side, led to growing interest in social welfare issues. Something had to be done to alleviate social conflict, to avoid a renewal of the revolution. The situation in which war orphans found themselves was terrible, especially in those cases where children of 'Red' families were taken from their mothers and put in the 'White' families of the victorious side. This usually meant removal from working class and urban homes in southern Finland and relocation in the more rural and conservative families in the north. Child welfare was seen at this time as the central task of poor relief. During the 1930s, much of the ideological influence in social welfare came from Germany. These influences included a streak of eugenics or 'racial hygiene'. The latter theories and practices were also growing in Sweden at this time, though they did not have any overt connection with fascist or Nazi ideology.

The third period of the history of social welfare in Finland can be located after the Second World War, when the foundations of a Nordic welfare state were established the modern social work profession was born. As in other Nordic countries, Finnish social work slowly developed as a professional practice from the administration of public poor relief. Firstly, the poor-house managers organised themselves and after a while started to educate themselves. The first short courses for poor relief workers were already operating in the 1890s. Some university level social welfare administration courses existed by the 1920s, when newly-independent Finland had a growing demand for educated carers and managers in social welfare.

Social work education itself started at university level in 1942 and initially German influence was very obvious (Satka, 1995). Finland had been allied with Germany in the Second World War. However, after the war there was an increase in American and British influence. Also the United Nations helped to develop Finnish social work practices. The concepts of social work adopted by Finland were those of a modern, democratic and American model, and found enthusiastic followers among some practising social welfare workers. However not all of them accepted the model of social casework, which appeared to over-emphasise the individual pathology of social problems. The most influential social welfare teacher, Professor Veikko Piirainen of Tampere University, fought strongly against this approach and, until his retirement at the end of the 1960s, modern social work theories were strongly resisted in university teaching. Only from the 1970s did this situation alter when social work literature on this began to be recognised in Finnish universities.

Municipalities as Service Producers

The Finnish Local Welfare State

The Nordic Welfare state model has some important features which affect social administration. European social care systems can be divided into four different models (Sipilä and Anttonen, 1996, p. 93).

- Countries with abundant social care services: Denmark, Sweden, and Finland;
- Countries with scarce social care services: Portugal, Greece, Spain, Ireland, and Germany;
- Countries with abundant services for elderly people but scarce services for children: the Netherlands, Norway, and Great Britain;
- Countries with abundant services for children but scarce services for elderly people: Belgium, France and Italy.

The Nordic welfare model of social service production is universalistic, meaning that all residents are entitled to social care services, regardless of their income or property. With such provision, the use of services tends not to be seen as stigmatising. Such universal services are produced largely if not entirely, through public funding, enabled by and reliant on a favourable economic climate. Currently, though there are fees for some services (about 10 per cent of costs are covered by fees) services are heavily supported by public finances.

If universalism is the first central feature of the Finnish social service model, the second important factor is the central role of local government in service production. There are certain fundamental differences between local government systems in Europe. Local government systems within the EU are usually categorised according to four models: the Nordic or Scandinavian model; the Central European model; the British model; and the South European or Napoleonic model (Niemi-Iilahti, 1995). The Finnish local government model is based on the principle of self-government. This principle is a centuries long Nordic tradition. It has also been incorporated into articles of the Finnish constitution since 1919. It is thus possible to speak of the municipalisation of the welfare state (Niemi-Iilahti, 1995) or of a local welfare state (Lehto, 1995) because of the pivotal role of local government in social service production. The common image of a Nordic welfare model based on a centralised state, as the service provider does not apply as, in Scandinavia, most public welfare and health care services are produced by municipalities. There is, however, a growing number of voluntary providers, whilst commercial services are virtually non-existent (Sipilä and Anttonen, 1996).

Another feature of the Finnish welfare model is that most of these organisations providing services are very small. As Table 8.1 shows, Finland has 455 municipalities, and about three-quarters, of them have less than 10,000 inhabitants.

Table 8.1 Municipalities according to the number of inhabitants in 1996

Inhabitants	Municipalities	Percentage
0 – 3,999	192	42
4,000 – 9,999	152	33
10,000 – 14,999	42	9
15,000-19,999	22	5
20,000-and above	47	10
Total	455	

Source: Facts about Finland, 1998, p. 5.

The small size of the municipalities means of course that social welfare administration in most of the cities is also small. In many smaller municipalities this might consist only of one social worker, her/his superior and some administrative support. In cities the situation is different: for example in Helsinki the social service personnel numbers some 10,000 workers, and the administrative staff is large. However, the general structure of the administration is the same across municipalities, regardless of their size, as indicated in Figure 8.1.

156 Management, Social Work and Change

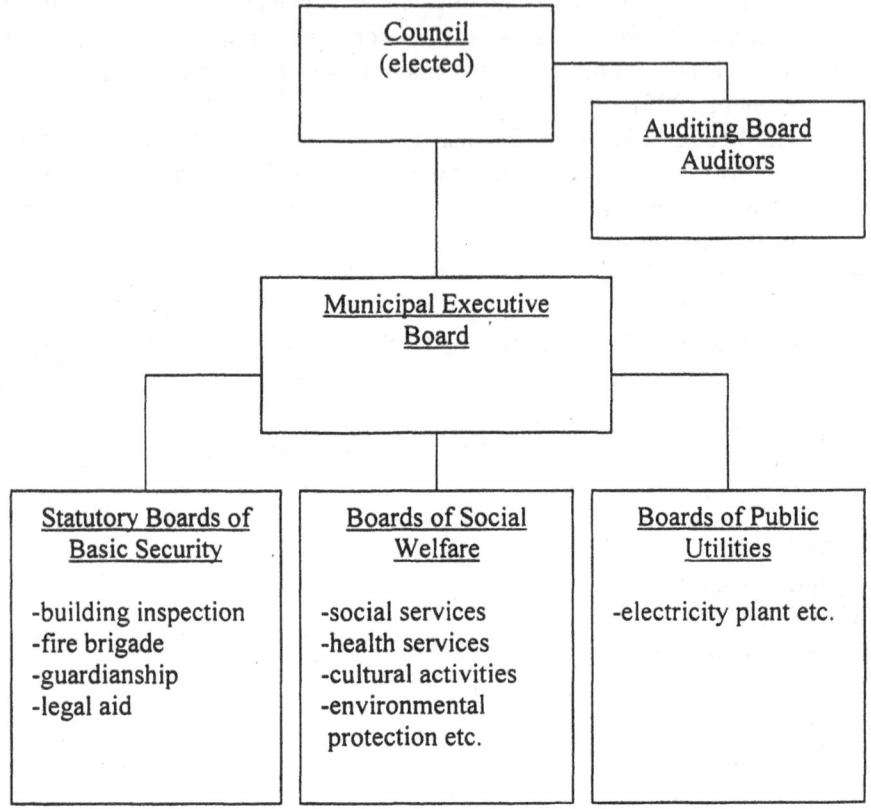

Figure 8.1 Organisational structure of Finnish local government

Social Welfare Administration

The central decision-making body in municipalities, the council, is elected every four years. The number of Council members varies according to the size of the municipality's population. The council nominates the municipal executive board and other boards. There are both statutory and optional municipal boards (Niemi-Iilahti, 1995). A board nominated by the city council formally manages social services administration in local governments. This board is generally known as the Board of Social Welfare, a name that directly reflects its function. The number of representatives depends on the size of the city but typically the board has eight members. Municipalities comprise both elected politicians and civil servants, as in UK local government. From the early 1980s the role of politicians in social welfare administration has diminished. This has led to a certain tension between professionals, administrators and politicians. There have been significant political difficulties in times of budgetary stringency, in reaching decisions which adequately reflect all views.

During recent years, 128 municipalities have combined their welfare and health care administration. Of these 128 municipalities, 65 made the decision to unite their social welfare and health care administrations during 1993, when the Finnish economy was in its deepest recession since the 1930s (Kuntaliitto, 1996). In 95 of these municipalities the administration has also been amalgamated (Kuntaliitto, 1996). In terms of the background of managers in these new combined welfare departments, they tend to be graduates and either social work or management professionals. In a 1996 survey, 23 per cent had a Master's degree in social work, 21 per cent were medical doctors and 15 per cent had a bachelor's degree in social work (Kuntaliitto, 1996). Combining two quite different organisational cultures has been a considerable challenge. There has been frequent professional conflict between health care and social welfare staff concerning leadership positions. According to an evaluation of 18 municipalities where both elected boards and welfare and health care offices have been amalgamated, this has resulted in possibilities both for strengthening co-operation between professionals and for re-organising the work of individual staff members throughout the organisation. Whilst the potential for greater so-operation has been recognised, this does not appear to have given rise to regular multi-disciplinary working. Nor did the mergers appear to reduce the running costs of social welfare and health care. According to this evaluation, staff numbers in social welfare diminished, whilst numbers in health care increased, resulting in a net effect on costs of zero (Rintala *et al.*, 1997).

Social Service Personnel

Service personnel in 1994 consisted of 650,000 persons, about 32 per cent of the total Finnish labour force (Ailasmaa and Ohtonen, 1997). Social service workers consist of approximately 13 per cent of the total labour force in service production. As Table 8.2 shows, the number of personnel in municipal social services has declined between 1991 and 1995 but the change is quite small. The most marked decline has been in children's day care personnel, where the drop is almost 9 per cent. Social service provision is seen largely as a caring, nurturing role and is traditionally regarded as belonging to the female domain. This is reflected in the gender breakdown of staff, showing 92 per cent of social service personnel are women (Ailasmaa and Ohtonen, 1997). Approximately 6 per cent of personnel work in social service management positions.

Table 8.2 The personnel in municipal social welfare services

	1991	1995
Children's day care	47,069	42,879
Institutional care for children	911	765
Other services for children	2,717	2,743
Residential care for elderly	17,542	11,679
Residential care for disabled	5,382	4,826
Rehabilitation and sheltered work	1,322	1,559
Home help service	11,757	13,174
Other services for elderly and disabled	346	489
Services for substance abusers	1,273	1,060
Social services total	**88,319**	**85,174**
Social welfare and health care administration	11,886	12,453

Source: Ailasmaa and Ohtonen, 1997, p. 190.

Finnish Social Workers

The general statistics about the workforce do not specify social workers as a separate professional group in social service personnel. According to a recent survey of all Finnish social workers (N = 3,638) (Marjamäki *et al.*, 1998), the ratio is one social worker to every 1,670 residents in municipalities. The government has accepted a recommendation that municipalities should provide social work services at a ratio of one worker to every 2,000 inhabitants. This recommendation appears to be fulfilled. However, cities in southern Finland (Helsinki, Tampere and Turku) employ a higher proportion than this, whilst in more rural areas there is a constant lack of social workers. Social workers are an ageing group, 65 per cent being aged 40 or over.

One of the most discussed topics in the Finnish social work debate has been the level of professionalisation of social workers. The educational level of social workers varies considerably. There are social workers with high level academic degrees, whilst others have no formal further or higher education (see Table 8.3). A policy objective written into statute in 1981 is for all social workers to be educated to MA level. As Table 8.3 shows, this aspiration has yet to be met. Although 73 per cent of social workers in social welfare offices have university level education, only 53 per cent have specific social work qualifications. The typical social worker's academic background is in social science, whilst others have qualifications in areas such as, pedagogy, theology or civil engineering. This educational profile demonstrates the tenuous level of professional status in social work currently. Whilst full professional status is the goal, there is considerable progress to be made before the claim can be legitimated entirely.

Table 8.3 The professional education of social workers (N = 3,658)

	Social workers		Total	
	(no.)	(%)	(no.)	(%)
PhD or licentiate	2		7	
Master of Science Degree	805	40	1,277	35
Bachelor of Science Degree	652	33	1,337	37
Polytechnic degree	12	1	30	1
Secondary degree	262	13	565	15
Other	107	5	225	6
No formal Education	151	8	217	6
Total	**1,991**	**100**	**3,658**	**100**

Source: Marjamäki et al., 1998).

Current Trends in Management

The following section evaluates current trends in Finnish social welfare administration. As noted earlier, influences on Fnnish social welfare administration formerly came from Sweden, Russia and Germany and latterly from Anglo-American models. Since the 1980s, Finnish social work administration has primarily been influenced by ideas from Sweden and the UK. British 'New Public Management' ideas, such as quality management, the purchaser/provider split and citizens' charters are all widely discussed and gaining acceptance in Finland. However, many of these ideas do not fit comfortably with Finnish administrative culture, with its strong belief in the power of public administration and its ideology of universal provision, which is at variance with ideologies from other countries.

Management Ideologies Since the 1950s

From recent research of Finnish social welfare managers (Aaltonen, 1997), management approaches from the early 1950s fall into three different periods. From the early 1950s to mid 1960s, welfare administration in municipalities was organised according to Tayloristic principles of work design, division of work and of specific job descriptions. During this period, power within social administration was concentrated in local social administration boards and their chairpersons. The boards were structured in a traditional bureaucratic form, with boards of directors and, in larger municipalities, several departments or divisions. These boards were strict in ensuring that rules and procedures were adhered to (Aaltonen, 1997). Whilst this may be seen as a period of classic bureaucratic rule, it is important to note that the politicians elected to serve on these boards had far more power than the administrative staff. Thus, decisions regarding the provision of particular services were largely taken by politicians. Administrative staff then implemented these decisions.

The period from 1966 to 1983 can be seen as a period of supplementation of the welfare state, where bureaucratic control of service production was evident, but where professionals had a growing importance. The social work profession helped define procedures in social administration. However, organisational structures were still hierarchical and divisionalised. Politically elected boards slowly lost their central role as decision-makers, to social administration staff. Social administration boards were considered more as supporters and regulators of professional staff than as managers of welfare work. Aaltonen (1997) considers this period as one seeing the transition from classical bureaucratic organisation, to a form of organisation in which professional administration came to the fore. Thus, a professional bureaucracy developed (Mintzberg, 1983), as professionals within social administration gained more status (Aaltonen, 1997).

The third period from 1984 to the present has seen a review and redefinition of the Finnish welfare state. Finland was again influenced by developments abroad, as the concept of managerialism grew in other countries. The features of professional bureaucracy slowly gave way to fresh ideas of new public management (Aaltonen, 1997). An initial manifestation of this was the introduction of a 'management by results' approach, after which a variety of other concepts, such as, quality management, citizens' charters and human resource management, were introduced. The following section examines the impact of the management by results approach and that of quality management.

Management by Results

Discussion of the role of municipalities in service production led to a large-scale development (viewed very much as an experiment) where state control was reduced, allowing greater autonomy for municipalities, in the provision of basic education, social and health care services. This 'free commune experiment' ran from 1989 to 1996 and paid particular attention to targeting and goal setting for services. This 'experiment' involved 56 municipalities (Niiranen, 1995). This trial took place at the time when the management by results ideology was at its strongest in municipal management. The specific purpose of this experiment was to decrease the hierarchical structure within city administration and to allow staff more scope to develop their own initiatives in providing services. It was thought this could be achieved by introducing such a culture. The managing by results approach had three main phases: establishing goals, allocating resources, and evaluating the results (Aaltonen, 1997). In evaluating this approach, Aaltonen found that this approach had been received positively. Of the managers surveyed, 79 per cent felt that management by results had clarified the goal-setting process: 64 per cent felt that the implementation had reduced bureaucracy and had increased the ability of staff to direct their own work. Further, 43 per cent of managers said that the management by results orientation has led to greater results-oriented leadership and in more efficient allocation of resources (Aaltonen, 1997). Aaltonen's findings appear to give strong support to the promises given by this approach in 1989. However, empirical research on the actual processes and outcomes of this approach at workplace level is still scarce.

In the second half of the 1990s, support for the management by results ideology began to wane. Whilst such an approach was seen to have some value, its applicability within social administration is limited. The complexity of welfare delivery and the difficulty of assessing outcomes, together with the long term nature of much welfare provision (Drucker, 1993; Eliassen and Kooiman, 1993) indicate that this approach could never be sustained as a comprehensive management approach. Managers began to look at other, more applicable, management concepts and that of quality management held much attraction.

Quality Management

The concept of quality management has been introduced with some success in the health care sector in Finland. As a result of this positive experience, managers in social services were keen to assess its suitability within their own working context. Cities, whose social services and health care services were combined in a single administration, facilitated a ready transfer of experiences of health care managers to the social services context. Evidence from the studies in the health care sector seems to suggest that it is easier to establish a quality management project in a big organisation, such as a hospital, than in smaller units, such as primary health care centres or social welfare offices. This appears to be largely a result of the resource requirements for establishing such an approach.

Regarding social services specifically, we do not yet have a national survey of the scope and impact of quality management. However, a survey was carried out to examine the implementation and extent of quality management initiatives (Mäntysaari, 1997). Interviews were conducted between March and June 1996 in 49 municipalities. More than 60 per cent of municipalities had implemented quality initiatives. The results are similar to those of Voutilainen *et al.* (1994) from primary health care centres. However, the social services results must be treated with some caution as they include minor quality initiatives in addition to more wide-scale developments. Thus, quality management may not have developed as extensively as may at first appear. Large-scale quality initiatives within social services do not appear to be widespread. However, it would appear that the Finnish social welfare system is continuing to adopt the concept of quality management. By 1998, the concept had become accepted in most municipalities as a legitimate management approach within social welfare. Empirical research on the actual effects of quality management is even more scarce than research on management by results. Recent research indicates that quality assessment is indeed widespread in social services but that an important element is being overlooked, namely that service users themselves are not taken into account in these developments. This may be due to continued professional domination of needs assessment, or to unresponsive organisational structures. Again it may be due to service users not being seen as equal partners in the provision and consumption of social services (Aaltonen, 1999).

Developments in Finland have followed a similar course with those in other countries. Management has had an increased profile and managers have instituted reforms and introduced new concepts. These have largely been accepted as having some relevance, as noted above. The process of management reform also has some similarities with experiences in other countries. New techniques and approaches have been introduced on a wide scale. They have not been introduced through using pilot schemes in some areas to assess their impact and relevance before introduction on a wider scale. Rather they have reflected the general interest in management and in new management approaches and the increased power associated with the management role.

Conclusions

During the 1990s an impressive structural change and reorganisation of social services has occurred in Finland. An economic downturn has been weathered. The economic recession led to a review of staff, resulting in their more effective utilisation in service provision. Local autonomy of service providers is stronger than in preceding decades. The 1990s have seen higher levels of unemployment. The resulting increased demand for welfare services, along with the general economic situation, have brought the universalist principles of the Finnish welfare state into question. Structural change has allowed the possibility of more wide-spread privatisation and the development of markets in social care (Lehto, 1995). These must, however, be viewed with some caution in that markets create their own difficulties within the context of social care (Wistow *et al.*, 1996). Further influences from abroad bring new challenges to social welfare administration. During the last few years these challenges have been presented in the forms of new public management approaches from UK and other parts of Europe, and in the a variety of 'third way' ideologies now also popular in the UK, the USA and Germany.

The incorporation of these influences within the Finnish context can be made without abandoning the central idea of the Nordic welfare state, that is, the idea of local service production, where the goals and guidelines of services are set by local decision-makers, within a national social policy framework. In this respect the Nordic model of service production is in line with resource dependency theories of organisation: organisations survive if they can adapt to local circumstances and modify their modes of action according to changes in the environment of the organisation.

The long history of poor relief and social services can present a considerable force for conservatism and is a potential source of strong resistance to the modernisation of service provision. Indeed, some of the principles and practices of new public management need to be treated with caution. However, there is sufficient positive value in these recent and continuing developments to suggest that further review of management and management practices is worthwhile. The increasing responsibility for services to be provided locally in response to local need is an important trend. This general principle is in accordance with the age-old Nordic principle of local responsibility and communitarian care of one's next-door neighbour.

References

Aaltonen, E.S. (1997), 'Sosiaalitoimen johtamisen organisaatioteoreettinen tarkastelu' (Organizational Study of Management within Municipal Social Administration), *Hallinnon tutkimus*, vol.16, no.3, pp. 225-36.

Aaltonen, E.S. (1999), 'Client Oriented Quality Assessment within Municipal Social Services', *International Journal of Social Welfare*, vol. 8, no. 2, pp. 131-42.

Ailasmaa, R. and Ohtonen, J. (1997), 'Sosiaali- ja terveyspalvelujen henkilöstö', in H. Uusitalo and M. Staff (eds), *Sosiaali-ja terveydenhuollon palvelukatsaus*, Raportteja, 214, Stakes, Helsinki.

Drucker, P. (1993), *Managing the Non-Profit Organization*, Butterworth Heinemann, Oxford.

Eliassen, K.A. and Kooiman, J. (1993), *Managing Public Organizations: Lessons From Contemporary European Experience*, Sage, London.

Facts about Finland (1998), *Facts about Finnish Social Welfare and Health Care*, Stakes, Helsinki.

Kuntaliitto (1996), *Kuntien sosiaali- ja terveystoimen hallinto*, Suomen Kuntaliitto, Helsinki.

Lehto, J. (1995), 'Adaptation or a New Strategy? Finnish Local Welfare State in the 1990s', *Finnish Local Government Studies (Kunnallistieteellinen aikakauskirja)*, vol. 23, no. 4, pp. 303-13.

Mäntysaari, M. (1997), 'Quality Management In Finland – Problems and Possibilities', in A. Evers, R. Haverinen, K. Leichensring and G. Wistow, *Developing Quality in Social Services: Concepts, Cases and Comments*, Ashgate, Aldershot.

Marjamäki, P., Mäntysaari, M. and Ristimäki, T. (1998), *Sosiaalityöntekijät Suomessa 1998. Tehtävät, Koulutus, Määrä ja Riittävyys (Social Workers in Finland 1998)*, Selvityksiä fin, no. 9, Ministry of Social Welfare and Health, Helsinki.

Mintzberg, H. (1983), *Structure in Fives: Designing Effective Organizations*, Prentice Hall, Englewood Cliffs.

Niemi-Iilahti, A. (1995), 'The Structure and Finance of Finnish Local Government in European Perspective', *Finnish Local Government Studies (Kunnallistieteellinen aikakauskirja)*, vol. 22, pp. 272-85.

Niiranen, V. (1995), 'The Multidimensional Management of Social Services', *Finnish Local Government Studies, (Kunnallistieteellinen aikakauskirja)*, pp. 421-22.

Rauhala, P.L. (1996), 'Miten Sosiaalipalvelut Ovat Tulleet Osaksi Suomalaista Sosiaaliturvaa?' *477 of Acta Universitatis Tamperensis ser A*, Tampereen yliopisto, Tampere.

Rintala, T., Elovainio, M. and Heikkilä, M. (1997), 'Osiensa Summa: Tutkimus Sosiaali-ja Terveydenhuollon Yhdistämisen Taustoista ja Vaikutuksista (The Sum of Its Parts: Study on the Background Factors, and the Effects of Combining Social Welfare and Health Care)' in series *Tutkimuksia*, no. 75, Stakes, Helsinki.

Satka, M. (1995), *'Making Social Citizenship: Conceptual Practices from the Finnish Poor Law to Professional Social Work'*, SoPhi, Helsinki.

Sipilä, J. and Anttonen, A. (1996), 'European Social Care Services. Is it Possible to Identify Models?', *Journal of European Social Policy*, vol. 6, pp. 87-100.

Voutilainen, P., Soveri, P. and Sairanen, S. (1994), 'Terveydenhuollon laadun kehittämisen nykytila Suomessa', (The Current Situation in Quality Assurance in Health Care), *Dialogi*, pp. 17-19.

Wistow, G., Knapp, M., Hardy, B., Forder, J., Kendall, J. and Manning, R. (1996), *Social Care Markets: Progress and Prospects*, Open University Press, Buckingham.

9 In Search of Legitimacy: Social Work Management in Hong Kong

VICTOR C.W. WONG AND SAMMY W.S. CHIU

Introduction

If social security is discounted, the bulk of government funded social welfare services in Hong Kong are provided by non-governmental organisations (NGOs), which currently receive some 76 per cent of total government expenditure on social welfare services. These NGOs, amounting to some 170, receive funding from the Social Welfare Department (SWD) and together provide services in six major areas: elderly and medical; family and child welfare; rehabilitation; young people; offenders; and lastly, community development. They employ about 80 per cent of all social welfare personnel and provide around 90 per cent of direct welfare services in Hong Kong. NGOs vary considerably both in size and the amount of money received from the Department. The top 15 NGOs together receive approximately half the total available funding (Coopers and Lybrand, 1995; Social Welfare Department, 1998).

The important role played by the NGOs in the delivery of social welfare or social work services is highlighted by the funding review exercise (also known as the subvention review exercise) conducted in March 1995. Coopers and Lybrand were commissioned to evaluate the existing social welfare funding system, through which the government finances and monitors NGOs. Three reports of the findings were published between July 1995 and August 1997. It was concluded that, from the SWD's point of view, the existing system did not work well, particularly with respect to the promotion of flexibility in service provision, accountability and performance monitoring. To improve the system, Coopers and Lybrand proposed to change the existing 'partnership' relationship between the government and the NGO sector to that of a clear-cut funder and provider. The former would 'set standards of performance, to provide funding and to monitor delivery', whilst the latter would 'deliver services to the agreed standards' (Coopers and Lybrand, 1995).

Regarding quality and accountability, two important measures are now being introduced: firstly, a formal funding and service agreement, which clearly specifies the nature, scope and quantity of services to be provided, and secondly, a new performance monitoring system. The NGOs did not disagree with these proposals, but at the same time, there was some concern that the measures might work against the principle of 'partnership' that had defined the relationship between the government and the NGOs. Would this lead to tension between the government and NGOs? In addition, there was some anxiety that the new system, with its managerial emphasis, might reduce the democratic and collective participation of service users. Would it reduce the potential for innovative social work practice and reduce social work to a remedial service only?

There are certainly no easy answers to such questions. But one thing is quite obvious, in the midst of social change, the government has been eager to alter its relations with the NGO sector. Alterations apply particularly to the provision and monitoring of social work and welfare services. Crucial to all this is the funding system. The rising importance of management in social work cannot, therefore, be isolated from an examination of this funding system nor from the overall nature of the relationship between the government and NGOs. This is explored in this chapter by means of two interlocking themes: the way in which legitimacy in social work and the government is constructed and the potential that exists for governmental control and exploitation. The chapter ends with a consideration of the way in which some of the changes may be beneficial for social welfare and social work.

Social Welfare in Hong Kong: A Brief Introduction

Hong Kong was a British colony until 1 July 1997 when it was restored to China. At this point it became China's Special Administrative Region. Social work services were developed in the British colonial era and are now framed in Basic Law, which is the mini-constitution governing the territory. Social welfare services in Hong Kong have developed significantly since the end of the Second World War. Over the past 20 years, government spending on social welfare has doubled from 9.1

billion Hong Kong dollars in 1977 to 18.2 billion in 1997. Alongside the increase of welfare spending, the scope of social welfare services has also expanded. Early social welfare services focused mainly on providing services to the less fortunate groups in the society and social problems such as poverty, child abandonment and prostitution were tackled (Chow, 1986). At present, social welfare services are provided across a wide spectrum: family and child welfare; services for young and elderly people; rehabilitation services for offenders; community development, as well as social security.

Notwithstanding the discernible growth of social welfare, two important features have to be noticed. Firstly, Hong Kong is not a Western type of welfare state, and it is argued that it should never become so (Chow, 1997). Indeed, in spite of the sizeable increase of social welfare spending, Hong Kong state welfare can still be regarded as minimal. Public expenditure in general and social welfare expenditure in particular, share only around 18 per cent and 5 per cent respectively of Hong Kong's total GDP. It has always been a government objective to promote family responsibility and social welfare has been construed as the last port of call. This feature of Hong Kong's social welfare system is clearly documented in the most recent social welfare White Paper:

> The family unit is a vital component of society ... The family is a source of support and strength in the care of the infirm and the elderly as well as disabled persons and the delinquent for whom family involvement generally contributes to a more successful rehabilitation. In Hong Kong, high values continue to be attached to the family unit to an extent which cannot be matched by any other institution (Hong Kong Government, 1991, p. 19).

For some time the government has been anxious that traditional family values and Chinese culture might be weakened or disrupted by delinquency, divorce and dependency on welfare. Hence, social welfare must be provided in ways that enhance the traditional values of self-reliance and respect for family obligations.

The second feature of the welfare system concerns the division of labour between the Hong Kong Government, the SWDs and the non-governmental organisations (previously known as voluntary agencies). Historically, voluntary agencies (VAs) were the pioneers of social welfare in Hong Kong. Funded primarily by overseas donations in the 1940s and 1950s, VAs provided the major welfare services. Subsequent to the rapid growth of the Hong Kong economy in the 1960s and 1970s, and the reduction in overseas funding, the Hong Kong Government gradually increased its role in welfare, primarily in terms of subsidising services that were provided by VAs. Partnership characterised the relationship between the SWDs and the NGOs. The former provided the welfare funding and the latter provided the actual services. VAs or NGOs are still the major providers of welfare services. They attract two thirds of total social welfare expenditure (social security discounted), and employ 80 per cent of professional social workers, welfare workers and child care workers in the territory.

The Relationship Between the Government and NGOs

Relationships between the NGOs and the Hong Kong Government can be traced back to the late 1940s, where, as noted earlier, voluntary agencies were the main providers of welfare services. In 1948, the Secretariat for Chinese Affairs set up a specialised unit, the Social Welfare Office to provide guidance and co-ordination of charitable work provided by philanthropic and voluntary organisations. According to the government of the day, the Social Work Office served as: 'the link between the government and the organisations' (Hong Kong Government, 1952, p. 79). All co-operation between the government and the voluntary sector in promoting social welfare in Hong Kong was considered at length in the first ever Social Welfare White Paper published in 1965. In this paper the government recognised the unique role played by the VAs as pioneers of social services and as major providers of social welfare services. But the White Paper also noted the tendency of the government to assume increasing responsibility in the social welfare field (Hong Kong Government, 1965).

In the early 1970s the government began to appreciate the benefit of 'a vigorous and progressive voluntary sector' (Hong Kong Government, 1973). Partnership was the principle that informed the government's relationship with the voluntary sector. There were three main reasons why it was important to maintain the strength of the VAs and to promote partnership. Firstly, voluntary social services can provide a basis of comparison with government services and stimulate mutual improvement. Secondly, voluntary agencies, being less bureaucratic than government departments, can be more flexible in pioneering new programmes to meet rising needs in the community. Thirdly, voluntary agencies can succeed in mobilising community resources, both in terms of volunteers as well as local and overseas donations (Kwan, 1986).

The 1979 White Paper on Social Welfare reiterated the importance of this partnership. However, there was a note of unease which had not been evident previously. The White Paper called for a clearer delineation of the division of responsibility between the government and the VAs (Hong Kong Government, 1979). For the voluntary sector, the major source of dissatisfaction was the bureaucratic and inflexible machinery of the funding system. More recently (Hong Kong Government, 1991), the government suggested that the maintenance and development of this partnership 'will require an on-going fostering of mutual understanding and trust' (Hong Kong Government, 1991, p. 18). This statement reflects an increasing dissatisfaction with the relationship between the two parties.

Partnership or an Increasingly Unequal Relationship

Although the government thought a partnership with the VAs or NGOs would be ideal, tensions have arisen due to the unequal status of the two parties. Regardless of any consultation, it is entirely up to the government to make the final decision with regard to policy on social welfare. Most important of all, the control of financial resources is entirely in the hands of the government. As a result, the sector is left with little choice but to follow all the guidelines the government provides. Since the 1980s, the voluntary sector has become increasingly dependent on government money and most VAs' services are now fully funded. This increases the government's control of VAs and undermines their potential for radical innovation (Chow, 1997). The clash between the two parties reflects fundamental differences in the definition of role and status: the government assumes a higher status in the control of subvention and service provision while the NGO sector wants to have a genuine partnership based on equal status. This struggle has jeopardised the trust between the two parties and led to the commissioning of Coopers and Lybrand to review the subvention system.

Arm's Length Provision of Services

As indicated above, VAs or NGOs are considered to be more flexible than government agencies, both in terms of the mobilisation of financial and human resources, and in the implementation of pioneering projects. Hence, VAs are valuable to the government and by keeping itself at a distance from direct provision, the government can overcome the constraints imposed by its own bureaucracy; for example, volunteers' and carers' support can be harnessed.

Additionally, by acting as a monitor of projects pioneered by the NGOs, the government can test community opinion and observe the practical and technical implications before it finally decides to commit itself to funding a particular service. Thirdly, the NGOs can be used as a vehicle for making changes along the direction desired by the government. For example, a working group was appointed by the government in 1993 to review child and youth centre services. As a result of the review, the centres were asked to refocus their services towards the disadvantaged and at-risk. The child and youth centres were also required to implement a set of performance indicators in the provision of core services defined by the government. These services are: guidance and counselling, supportive services for young people in disadvantaged circumstances, socialisation programmes, and social responsibility enhancement programmes (Working Group on Reviewing Child and Youth Centre Services, 1993; Working Group on Implementation Guide to Report on the Review of Child and Youth Centre Services, 1994). Finally, the separation of financing from the provision of services strengthens the legitimacy of the government. By overseeing and monitoring the service provided by the NGOs, the government maintains arm's length control on the one hand, and uses the NGOs as a buffer against public criticism on the other.

A Case of Control and Exploitation?

Once an NGO becomes a government financed agency it is subjected to direct and indirect control from the government even if it remains privately owned. It has to abide by government rules regarding financial procedures and reimbursement. The SWD has the power to monitor the financial conditions of the agency and make changes to the monthly or quarterly cash advances. Also, even though the NGO staff are not civil servants, the agencies have to apply their pay scales. Furthermore, agencies are not allowed to exceed the quotas for new personnel unless the salaries of the new recruits are totally financed by the agency itself. Regarding the recruitment of social work staff to a government funded post, the NGO has to follow strictly the employment requirements of the SWD. In other words, only those employees who possess qualifications recognised by the SWD are approved.

Hence, NGOs are subject to strict financial and personnel control by the government. Against this background, however, the staff of NGOs enjoy inferior fringe benefits in housing, leave and pensions, compared to their counterparts in the government. Promotion opportunities are limited in NGOs since there are fewer senior posts. The incorporation of NGOs into the social welfare service system has enabled the government to exercise control on the one hand, yet exploit differences concerning fringe benefits and extra resources on the other.

In the 1970s and 1980s, social workers in Hong Kong were aware of the socio-political dimension of need and those in community work settings were active in using social action to advance grassroots welfare (Wong, 1993; Kwok et al., 1995). However, the government has proposed the phasing out of funded community development projects which were set up for the deprived and transient. This proposal has incited criticism from the social work profession for two reasons. Firstly, these community development projects only involved 0.3 per cent of annual government spending, and secondly, the increasing polarisation of wealth has contributed to the spread of deprivation in both new towns and inner urban areas (Chiu and Wong, 1998a).

The battle for the maintenance of these community projects continues, but whether the government would be happy to fund projects that might produce political pressure upon itself is yet to be seen (Chiu, 1996). Also, as discussed earlier, services are being refocused with regard to children and young people. There is growing concern that the service has become too individually focused (Wong and Chiu, 1998; Wong and Shiu, 1998). Indeed, an empirical study revealed that mediation and remedial social work practice has been reinforced during the recent political transformation (Chiu and Wong, 1997; 1998a). Despite, or perhaps because of the above, the government seems increasingly afraid of losing control over service direction.

Controversies Over the 'Unit Grant Funding' Proposal

One of the major controversies over the management of relations between the government and NGOs is the 'unit grant funding' proposal. Such a proposal has significant implications for both financial control and human resources management within NGOs. Under the proposed fixed funding formula, the finances of each service unit can be managed and used by NGOs with much more flexibility. Free virement between the spending items can occur and no claw back of unspent funds takes place. The government will amend the funding in line with the annual civil service salary adjustment, but it will make no further provision for incremental payments, nor will it allow top-up for deficits. The NGO sector is particularly against this proposal for three major reasons. Firstly, NGOs found the proposed subvention level for salary and fringe benefits unacceptable as it is biased against those agencies with the majority of their staff members at the top of their salary scales (Hong Kong Council of Social Service, 1997). On the implementation of the new funding proposal, NGOs will risk running into the red, particularly in view of the low rate of wastage and resignation within the sector at the moment. Secondly, according to the new proposal, the existing service units could opt for maintaining the current funding system while new service units or projects must comply with new regulations. The case of 'One Agency, Two Systems' could take place and this is likely to create difficulty and confusion (Law, 1997). Finally, less than half of the some 170 governmental financed agencies in Hong Kong were provided with money for central administration. Without the provision of extra financial support the small to medium size agencies will find it difficult to cope with the more complex task of financial control induced by the new funding system itself.

The SWD (1997) argues that the new system is better because it allows agencies to de-link from civil service pay scales and recruit staff who are not social work trained. In addition, the new system offers NGOs flexibility over contracting out and hiring part-time or temporary staff. However, the social work profession has been sceptical about this so-called advantage. The profession fears that the introduction of the new system will erode the quality of social work or social welfare service. At the same time, the separation from civil service pay scales, salaries and fringe benefits may further undermine conditions of service.

The controversy over the new funding mechanism is by no means over. It will remain a hot issue for social work professionals and managers. Despite the debate, the two-track system in which the government takes advantage of the funded agencies yet strictly controls them will continue. The current questions revolve around the extent of exploitation and whether the conflicts between the government and NGO sector will increase.

In Search of Legitimacy Through Management

A reordering of the relationship between the government and NGOs is central to the whole funding review exercise. In the eyes of the government, the continuation of partnership with NGOs would perpetuate an impression of equality that the government would very much like to avoid. Indeed, the SWD's approach towards the NGO sector has become increasingly negative in recent years. The sector is seen as 'increasingly politicised' and it has 'focused on obtaining more resources without specific reference to the consequent effect on service levels' (Coopers and Lybrand, 1995, p. 7). This perception suggests that the financing of social welfare services has become an acute political and economic issue. Underlying the government's concern has been the NGO's increasing demands for more resources and their pressure for a growing array of rights to welfare services (Chiu, 1996; Wong, 1996; Chiu and Wong, 1998b). In order to keep these problems under control, the SWD has introduced the funder/provider relationship as a replacement of the previous partnership. The new relationship makes the government both funder and monitor of NGOs. Resulting from this change, the government assumes the responsibility to 'ensure adequate accountability for the expenditure of public funds' and 'to assess individual NGO performance' (Coopers and Lybrand, 1995, p. 29). Thus, the legitimacy of reshaping the relationship is in the public interest as the proper use of government revenue is ensured. In other words, without taking such a 'critical' step to reorder the relationship with the NGOs, the proper use of public funds may not be guaranteed.

However, NGOs have a different view of the changes. NGOs worry that the new relationship will give the government increased legitimacy to exercise control (Hong Kong Council of Social Services, 1997), and that this may result in a further loss of creativity and initiative in the provision of social services.

Funding and Service Agreements: Redefining the Boundaries

The funder/provider relationship between the government and the NGO sector has been formalised by the introduction of the Funding and Service Agreement (FSA) and the system of quality standards. The stated objective of the Agreement is, 'to set out the basis on which the SWD and each NGO agrees, respectively, to fund and to operate a social welfare services' (Coopers and Lybrand, 1996, p. 25). Although the agreement is of an informal and non-legal character, it is intended to be the means of defining the areas in which the SWDs and NGOs are accountable for performance. Under the current subvention system the NGOs have to observe the service-specific policy objectives and compile the necessary financial and service statistics for the SWD. However, beyond these obligations they are 'entrusted' to provide services and to respond in accordance with their professional judgement to emerging need. The introduction of FSA is an attempt to document the relations between the SWD and NGOs in order to 'clarify expectations and define the boundaries of flexibility in service delivery' (Coopers and Lybrand 1996, p. 26). The redefinition of flexibility enjoyed by NGOs is thus considered by the government to be a 'logical' consequence of the reshaping of the relationship. The NGO sector is openly against the erosion of a relationship based on partnership but it can not afford to resist the introduction of the agreement for two interlocking reasons. Firstly, NGOs would invite public criticism if they resisted the idea of promoting greater accountability in the use of public funds, and secondly, the sector is largely dependent on the provision of government funding for service operation.

The agreement consists of four major parts: (1) the nature, purpose and objectives of the service to be provided; (2) the performance standards to be achieved; (3) the obligations of the SWD to service operators; and (4) the basis of subvention. A major concern of the NGOs involves the output requirement of FSAs. Such requirements can radically alter the nature and quantity of service output. Family Life Education (FLE) provides an example. FLE is categorised by the SWD as part of the family and child welfare service, which is mostly run by the NGO sector. Although the scope of the FLE service has been revised over the past ten years, the fundamental philosophy of promoting and sustaining the 'family as a unit' has been retained (Lo, 1997). In addition to stipulating married couples as the primary target group of the service, the SWD also specifies the format of programmes, the quantity of services to be provided, the level of efficiency, and the time scale in which plans should be achieved. These requirements have imposed two restrictions. Firstly, by needing to fulfil the required quantitative output the NGOs have to target participants who will readily participate, for example, housewives and young people. This means men, older people and other minority groups become a lower priority. Secondly, since the provision of services is so closely tied up with the availability of funding and the service nature is so narrowly defined by the SWDs, there is little room for innovative, radical practice. Moreover, the introduction of FSAs may be used as a tool to reduce public criticism of the government. For example, when the government was criticised for not offering services to the new Chinese immigrants, the SWD asked the NGO sector to make a response based on the stipulations of the FSA. By so doing, the NGO sector then becomes a buffer that absorbs public criticisms on behalf of the government.

The government has also directly placed specific service expectations on the NGOs for youth work. To ensure that these expectations are translated into practice, the government defines services that are provided to at-risk youths as 'core' and these in turn receive higher priority both in service implementation and in funding. Core services depend on individualised definitions of problems; for example, gang behaviour, triad involvement, misuse of drugs, school drop-outs, sex-related problems, and poor parent-child relationships (Chiu and Wong, 1998b). Services are then divided into mainstream and peripheral with the former being seen as more important for funding purposes. The construction of a mainstream youth service encourages NGOs to run such 'core' services not only to assure subvention but also as a means of service expansion in the future. However, this influences the definition of the needs of young people and solutions are seen as lying with NGOs or young people themselves. Hence, tighter control over the content and quantity of service has shifted the pressure onto the service providers and obscured the political responsibility of the government in tackling the structural causes of social problems. Service delivery is more tightly linked to policy laid down by the government and the FSA ensures compliance. This, in turn, unnecessarily erodes the capacity of NGOs to make radical responses to community needs. Much time and energy will be consumed in achieving the 'basic' quantity requirements and 'peripheral' activities focused on non-target groups will not be recognised.

Quality Through Good Management

In keeping with the previous colonial regime, the new government of Hong Kong continues to rely on economic progress as the primary means of gaining credibility. Social policy and social welfare remain subordinate to economic development (Chiu and Wong, 1998b). The pursuit of value for money, efficiency, effectiveness and accountability has been a recurring theme as the government seeks to manage the tensions between rising welfare demands and the drive to contain the growth of public expenditure. 'Good management' lies at the heart of resolving the tension (Newman, 1998). Those in charge of service units, though mostly of social work background, are now largely identified as managers. Most important of all, the call for quality services has provided the government with the opportunity to manoeuvre the language of management into welfare organisations. Particular emphasis is now placed on performance assessment. As remarked in the management consultancy report, 'monitoring the performance of NGOs against the agreed performance standards will form a key role of the Government in relation to the NGO sector in the future' (Coopers and Lybrand, 1995, p. vi).

Quality Standards: Towards Increasing Managerial Control

Performance assessment depends on the setting of standards (Coopers and Lybrand 1995). The formulation of quality standards is based on four principles, namely, the provision of information, service unit management, services to clients and finally, respect for clients' rights. Accordingly, 19 standards and 79 criteria are drawn up under these major principles. What is important is that the protection and promotion of client or user rights is put forward as the cornerstone of quality service. Very few social work professionals would disagree with this principle. However, social work professionals and the government might disagree whether management is an effective solution to social welfare problems. An empirical study conducted by the authors shows that the social work respondents did not take agency management as an important function of social work practice. Instead, a large proportion of the respondents considered individual and group counselling as the most important (Chiu and Wong, 1997).

New ideas concerning quality management and performance assessment mean that each and every NGO is required to document, and make available for public scrutiny, the information concerning service provision. Because of the very heavy management work expected, these service quality standards are to be introduced in three phases over a period of approximately three years. The SWD, as a direct service provider, is also required under the new system to comply with the new service quality standards. But unlike the smaller or even medium-size NGOs in Hong Kong the SWD has many more resources upon which to draw. For the NGOs, the documentation of service information and social work activities has created an added burden. Extra resources to deal with these additional managerial requirements have to be sought once again from the government. So far the SWD has made no promise that extra resources will be forthcoming.

Once the NGOs have made a commitment to implementing the service quality standards, they will be assessed as to whether the standards have been met. There are two steps in the assessment process: a self-assessment conducted on an annual basis and an external assessment conducted by the SWD every three or four years. To enforce the managerial approach the SWD will also provide incentives and sanctions. Excellent NGOs or service units will be appraised as 'mentors' and those meeting the requirements of all the quality standards will be given an accredited status. Those who need some improvement in the quality control processes will be given transitional status. Resources and opportunities for service expansion may be given to the mentors, whilst those NGOs that show little progress may be sanctioned by the withdrawal of government funds.

In Hong Kong, social welfare organisations are expansion driven. Agency managers aim to increase services and expand the organisation. In this context the usual logic for the service managers is 'the bigger the organisation, the better the services'. As a result, the reputations of the welfare agencies and their managers depend very much on their ability to acquire new resources. Hence, quality management, which should safeguard the welfare of service users, might easily become an instrument in the struggle for increased budgets.

The consequences of implementing quality management are not just to do with workload, but also whether an organisation might expand or contract, or indeed, succeed or fail. Every NGO has to engage in activity recognised as valid by the assessor/funder and develop the necessary management skills for survival. However, it may be the case that when quality standards exist, organisational attention shifts from the original purpose of promoting the rights and welfare of the users to the procedures for providing the service. Thus, goal displacement may follow (Gummer, 1990). The self-assessment exercise undertaken by each service unit may also reinforce the co-opting of social work professionals into the management process. This may rapidly lead to the internalisation of new rules of management and assessment and help strengthen the subordination to managerial imperatives without reservation or resistance (Kirkpatrick and Lucio, 1995; Gray and Jenkins, 1997).

Management for Quality: Resistance and Way Out

Although quality management may be understood as state surveillance and political manipulation it may still be mediated at the organisational and practice levels. That means that positive change may be realised at the organisational level if managers and practitioners are wise enough to make the most of the opportunities that remain. Social work professionals can still reflect on the interplay between politics, managerialism and quality (James, 1994). Most important of all, the aim of quality management is to improve services and promote welfare. Thus, NGOs could take the introduction of service quality standards as an opportunity to facilitate wider user participation at the organisational level and promote user rights to welfare at the institutional or societal level.

However, quality management typically fails to recognise the power differentials between providers and users (Ian, 1995). Service users are particularly subject to control as they are usually located at the margins of society or they are involuntary users for whom the idea of choice has little meaning. As providers of social welfare services, social work professionals cannot afford to overlook the power dimension despite being subject to heavy workload and managerial pressures. Otherwise, service users may turn out to become victims of the tension that results from attempts to improve quality.

Quality standards are not restricted to practitioner-user interaction or to the point of service consumption. They also include the ideological and material aspects of service provision. Practitioners and users at the service unit level may disagree over the nature of the problem to be solved, the best way to a solution, or even both. More progressive NGOs campaign to change the circumstances which cause a social problem: for example, by advocating for changes of social policy, by raising awareness of service users or in persuading their own or other organisations to change their practice. Social work practitioners may also encourage users to put pressure on policy makers and to advocate for the redistribution of wealth and power. Not surprisingly, the 19 service quality standards do not facilitate a collective response to service provision. The individualistic discourse of quality service is concerned with meeting individual needs but fails to consider the structural or policy dimension of social problems. Redefining quality standards might be a way of promoting a collective perception of social welfare.

Conclusion

In the midst of social change in Hong Kong, the pursuit of flexibility, accountability and quality has legitimised the reshaping of the relationship between the government and the NGO sector. There are, however, continuities as well as changes in this relationship. Controversies over the funding policy will continue as both the government and the NGO sector are eager to shape the relationship in ways which favour their own party. There is an urgent need to understand the politics of quality and its links with the power dimension of service provision and the wider policy initiatives and structural imperatives. It is no longer possible to separate the social construction of quality and quality management from the political agenda of social welfare in the public sphere. Social work professionals must critically reflect on quality management as a means of ensuring that the rights of service users are enhanced.

References

Chiu, S.W.S. (1996), 'Social Welfare' in M.K. Nyaw and S.M. Li (eds), *The Other Hong Kong Report 1996*, The Chinese University Press, Hong Kong.

Chiu, S.W.S. and Wong, V.C.W. (1997), 'The Roles and Functions of Social Work in an Era of Political Transformation: The Case of Hong Kong', *Social Policy and Social Work*, vol. 1, no. 1, pp. 47-71.

Chiu, S.W.S. and Wong, V.C.W. (1998a), 'From Political to Personal? Changing Social Work Ideology and Practice in Hong Kong', *International Social Work*, vol. 40, no. 3, pp. 276-91.

Chiu, S.W.S. and Wong, V.C.W. (1998b), 'Social Policy in Hong Kong: from British Colony to Special Administrative Region of China', *European Journal of Social Work*, vol. 1, no. 2, pp. 231-42.

Chow, N.W.S. (1986), 'The Past and Future Development of Social Welfare in Hong Kong', in J. Cheng (ed.), *Hong Kong in Transition*, Open University Press, London.

Chow. N.W.S. (1997), 'A Critique of the New Subvention System', *Newsletter of the Diocesan Welfare Council*, no. 29, pp. 3-5 (in Chinese).

Coopers and Lybrand (1995), *Review of the Social Welfare Subvention System: report to the Investigatory Phase of the Review*, Coopers and Lybrand, Hong Kong.

Coopers and Lybrand (1996), *Review of Social Welfare Subvention System: Report of the Detailed Design Phase*, vol. 1 & 2, Coopers and Lybrand, Hong Kong.

Gray, A. and Jenkins, B. (1997), 'Markets, Managers and the Public Service: The Changing of a Culture', in P. Taylor-Gooby and R. Lawson (eds), *Markets and Managers: New Issues in the Delivery of Welfare*, Open University Press, Buckingham.

Gummer, B. (1990), *The Politics of Social Administration: Managing Organisational Politics in Social Agencies*, Prentice Hall, New Jersey.

Hong Kong Council of Social Service (1997), *Press Release: Welfare Agencies Against New Funding Proposal*, Hong Kong Council of Social Service, 26 September.
Hong Kong Government (1952), *Hong Kong Annual Report 1951*, Government Printer, Hong Kong.
Hong Kong Government (1965), *Aims and Policy for Social Welfare in Hong Kong: A White Paper*, Government Printer, Hong Kong.
Hong Kong Government (1973), *Social Welfare in Hong Kong: The Way Ahead*, Government Printer, Hong Kong.
Hong Kong Government (1979), *Social Welfare into the 1980s*, Government Printer, Hong Kong.
Hong Kong Government (1991), *Social Welfare into the 1990s and Beyond*, Government Printer, Hong Kong.
Ian, S. (1995), 'The Quality of Mercy: The Management of Quality in the Personal Social Services', in I. Kirkpatrick and M.M. Lucio (eds), *The Politics of Quality in the Public Sector: The Management of Change*. Routledge, London.
James, A. (1994), 'Reflections on the Politics of Quality', in A. Connor and S. Black (eds), *Performance Review and Quality in Social Care*, Jessica Kingsley Publishers, London.
Kirkpatrick, I. and Lucio, M.M. (1995), 'Introduction', in I. Kirkpatrick and M.M. Lucio (eds), *The Politics of Quality in the Public Sector: The Management of Change*, Routledge, London.
Kwan, A.Y.H. (1986), 'Social Welfare and Services in Hong Kong', in A.Y.H. Kwan and D.K.K. Chan (eds), *Hong Kong Society: A Reader*, Writers' and Publishers' Co-operative, Hong Kong.
Kwok, R.H.Y., Mok, H.T.K. and Leung, B.L. (eds) (1995), *Approaches to Community Work in Hong Kong*, China Book Company: Hong Kong (in Chinese).
Law, C.K. (1997), 'Review of the Subvention System: One Country, Two Systems', *Ming Pao Daily*, 12 December (in Chinese).
Lo, K.L.N. (1997), 'Parenting Education of Family Life Education in Hong Kong: Critique and Insights from Post-structuralist Perspectives', Unpublished MA Dissertation, University of Bradford.
Newman, J. (1998), 'Managerialism and Social Welfare', in G. Hughes and G. Lewis (eds), *Unsettling Welfare: The Reconstruction of Social Policy*, The Open University Press, London.
Social Welfare Department (1997), *Review of the Social Welfare Subvention System*. A Letter issued to chairperson/agency head of all subvented non-governmental organisations on 29 December, Social Welfare Department, Hong Kong.
Social Welfare Department (1998), *Social Welfare Department Annual Report for 1997-1998*, Government Printer, Hong Kong.
Wong, C.K. (1993), 'State-Funded Social Work Projects for Social Reform: Reflections on Community Organising in Hong Kong', *International Social Work*, vol. 36, pp. 249-60.
Wong, V.C.W. (1996), 'Medical and Health', in M.K. Nyaw and S.M. Li (eds), *The Other Hong Kong Report 1996*, The Chinese University Press, Hong Kong.
Wong, V.C.W. and Chiu, S.W.S. (1998), 'The Social Production of Marginality of Youth in Hong Kong: In the Eyes of Social Workers', *Youth Studies Australia*, vol. 17, no. 1, pp. 36-42.

Wong, V.C.W. and Shiu, W.K.C. (1998), The Structural is Personal? Re-examination and Re-development of Youth Work in Hong Kong, *Youth Studies Journal*, vol. 1, no. 2, pp. 198-207 (in Chinese).

Working Group on Implementation Guide to Report on Review of Children And Youth Centre Services (1994), *Implementation Guide to Report on Review of Children and Youth Centre Services*, Government Printer, Hong Kong.

Working Party on Review of Children and Youth Centre Services (1993), *Report on Review of Children and Youth Centre Services*, Government Printer, Hong Kong.

Conclusion: Emergent Themes

JOHN LAWLER

This book has developed a number of themes through the course of its constituent chapters. This concluding chapter highlights some of the transitions, tensions, paradoxes and dichotomies within and between these themes and considers the value of comparing social work developments in different contexts and the need for social work organisations to continue to adapt appropriately.

Foundations

In reviewing current social work policy, organisation and management it is important, as is increasingly demonstrated throughout the book, to consider the particular context under review. The foundations of social policy and the bases of the means to deliver social welfare services are complicated. One can see their development, not as the enactment of a strategic blueprint, working from a stable and agreed base, but as a set of policy directives - sometimes related, sometimes not - which in aggregate form a set of incremental changes. This process of development is evident both in Western states and in states evolving after the demise of communism. It has clearly happened in the UK, in spite of what might have been seen as a strategic outline provided by Beveridge in the 1940s. The report that bears his name is influenced by many contextual and historical developments. Indeed, such policy initiatives in all countries are significantly influenced by the expectations, beliefs and aspirations of many individuals and groups and by the resources available to operationalise policies. Underlying philosophies of welfare and definitions of social work, together with differing expectations of the role of state, individual and family will influence the development of policy and the way in which policy is translated into practice. Inevitably, as such developments occur within dynamic socio-political environments, compromises are reached or initiatives taken in the face of opposition. In reviewing developments in other contexts and in considering specific countries and the role of social work within them, we can see differences and commonalities. For evaluation of policy and for its future development, these merit further discussion. The book began with an introduction to developments from a perspective – postmodernisation – which recognises that we are witnessing a period of major transition in welfare in general and in social work in particular. This and the related approaches of postmodernism and post-structuralism, provide helpful analytical views from which to consider the current situation and its inherent tensions. Leonard (1997) and Parton (1994) make useful points in discussing the use of a postmodern perspective in analysing the development of welfare. Leonard highlights the aim of the modernity 'project' and its manifestation in organisational form:

> Order, rather than disorder and confusion, progress and innovation rather than stagnation under the sign of tradition and, above all, rationality rather than irrationality and superstition, these were the hallmarks of the discourse of modernity which has sedimented into concrete forms of practice: modern bureaucracy (Leonard, 1997, p. 87).

The consistency and rationality which bureaucratic organisation in welfare was expected to provide have instead led to inflexibility and insensitivity. Such organisations have not developed in such a way as to innovate in response to changing circumstance. Instead we are left with unexpected difficulties and uncertainties. The irony of this is noted by Parton (1994), who notes that we now live in:

> a world which has become disorientated, disturbed and subject to doubt .... characterised by the fragmentation of modernity into forms of institutional pluralism marked by variety, difference, contingency, relativism and ambivalence – all of which modernity sought to overcome (Parton, 1994, p. 10).

The means designed to deal with the uncertainties of previous eras have led to different uncertainties in the present. The themes of the opening chapter are echoed here as we consider the present situation and possible developments in the light of such perspectives.

The Statutory, Voluntary and Independent Sectors, the Community and the Family

We have seen how the concept of decentralisation is operating in social welfare. Policy makers in social care envisage the use of an increasing range of providers in delivering social work and other welfare services. We can also see how the combination of state or national provision, combines with more localised, regional provision, with voluntary organisations and with informal, domestic or family care. All have responsibilities in the provision of social care. Some of those responsibilities are declared in statute, others are implicit. The way in which these agencies are combined varies considerably from state to state and also from region to region. The Russian context is one with a recent history of comprehensive state provision. Hong Kong's history indicates a far greater reliance on voluntary organisations in the provision of welfare. In the UK we have seen and are witnessing now, how the relationships between the various parties involved are changing. There is no ideal combination. As a result of the variety of relationships and roles, generalised theories of social welfare organisation are of limited use (Klein, 1993). What appears an appropriate mix at one time may become inappropriate within an ever-changing context. Dominant views within social policy are seen to alter over time, for example, the role of the market in social care is now significant and is a radical departure from debates in the UK surrounding welfare delivery before the late 1980s (Wistow et al., 1996). One of the primary considerations in welfare development, regardless of how it is delivered, is whether services should be available to every citizen or whether conditions of eligibility should be introduced to target services.

Universal or Selective Provision – a Framework of Delegation

Whilst a universal view of humanity, and attendant rights and needs, gains increasing currency, policy tensions regarding how those human needs should be addressed continue. Should the aims of a welfare state include full employment? Should the aims of social work policy include the provision of universal or selective services? The indications are that the trend is to provide increasingly selective services. However, this does not indicate the demise of universal provision across the welfare domain. The UK still sees the provision of health and education as universal, albeit with the introduction of a different model of involvement and exchange – the increasing use of markets, quasi-markets and consumer choice. The development of such markets in welfare seen by some (for example, Mishra, 1993) as a sign that universal provision has been transcended by consumerism, choice and enterprise. As consumers begin to find their voice in contexts such as those discussed in earlier chapters, and to articulate their own needs rather than have them defined by the state, greater flexibility is called for. Different needs are emerging from different parts of the population. The altered definition of the user - from client to consumer – implies that diverse and individual needs must be addressed. Different groups and individuals have different stakes in the state, its welfare structure and in social work provision. The debate over universal or selective provision takes place within a context, both globally and within different nations, where a unitary approach to social provision is giving way increasingly to a pluralist view (Mishra, 1993). Policy, then, needs to take account of and balance the views, aspirations and expectations of diverse stakeholders. This pluralism is increasingly seen as likely to endure. It does not represent a transitional phase towards a new consensus or new unitarism. Policy makers need to take account of this and to reflect the different views and needs within society as well as accepting some of the contradictions which are inherent in planning within a pluralist scenario.

We are also seeing the growing distinction between social security and social work. In recent history these two elements of welfare have been combined, under both totalitarian (Russia) and democratic (Finland) states. As globalisation increases, so does the distinction between these two welfare elements. The trend reflected here again highlights the role of the citizen increasingly as individual and consumer and less as part of a collective whole. For this reason, services become more diversified and more distinct from one another. As responsibility for welfare rests increasingly on individuals and their families, the state moves away from universal provision and away from general and undifferentiated organisations with total responsibility for the assessment of need and the co-ordination and delivery of services. This reflects strongly the concepts of the dispersal dimension of decentralisation, seen as part of the postmodernisation thesis explored in the introductory chapter (O'Brien and Penna, 1998).

Equality and Diversity

Again we note an interesting development if not a paradox. State boundaries are becoming both more permeable (through developments such as EU, Schengen agreement) and more rigid, as nations wish to prevent increasing and unregulated immigration. Race and ethnicity are becoming more significant issues as boundaries are redefined. However, the actual multi-ethnic profile of many societies, particularly the UK, is insufficiently recognised, it is argued (Baldock, 1994), as the variety of cultural needs is not addressed by service provision. Race and ethnicity may have important parts to play in developing welfare frameworks in terms of the inclusion and exclusion of people for social work and other welfare services. Again there is an interesting contrast between collective identities formed on the basis of racial or religious affinities and the increasingly individualist character ascribed to citizens. The increased interest in equality of service and of opportunity stands in contrast to this. As the issue of equality has developed it has brought into sharp relief the inequality which exists in many areas of life and work, including, as we have seen, that of management. What the ensuing debates have usefully and clearly highlighted is the wealth of diversity. By considering, for example, the opportunity to become a manager, we have seen the different perspectives and experiences which are now available for analysis. These cause us to reflect on a healthy and positive diversity being unveiled in response to a perceived need to challenges institutional practices which reinforce discrimination. Such perspectives also cause us to call into question traditional views, for example, of management, which may have been presented in a uni-dimensional way, reflecting current hegemony. This then causes us to develop wider perspectives, a fuller understanding of the dilemmas and choices facing people. Leonard (1997) also highlights the need to take note of the different narratives taking place which stress different identities and to recognise the potential for 'solidarity' of interests which cut through the different discourses. Such a recognition does not, however, lead inevitably to a renaissance of monolithic institutions addressing only common need; flexibility and innovation in response to local conditions can still be taken into account.

Local and Global

We have examined the trend towards globalisation and its impact on social work thinking, policy and organisation. This is a trend which will undoubtedly continue. There is indeed an explicit wish from countries with less fully developed social work services to learn from the experience of (Western) countries as the pressure grows for an increase in the number and efficiency of services. We can see, for example through EU legislation, how social policy is beginning to transcend national boundaries. This pull towards globalisation is tempered by the need to focus services on the specific and diverse needs of local communities and individuals. In a strictly commercial free market this would be clarified by consumer power. However, the limitations of free markets in this context are considerable and the actions of agents on behalf of communities or vulnerable people present a different model for the allocation of resources. We are not faced, as indeed is the case with many of these tensions, with a choice of either globalisation or localisation: we are faced with *both* globalisation *and* localisation. Policy makers, managers and professional have balances to make in deciding the nature and form of service in response to these very different influences. We are witnessing dispersal, localisation and fragmentation, in a framework of rapid transnational communication, mobility, competition and resources transfer. How social work managers and practitioners operate in this context requires further debate.

Manager and Professional

The role of the professional social worker is clearly subject to different forces. At one level, for example in Russia, we see the evidence of the struggle for the establishment of the social work profession and for its credibility and legitimacy. In the UK we can see how this professional social work status and its attendant autonomy are under threat or in conflict with the role of manager. The rise of managerialism has seen greater decision-making authority and status invested in the manager's role at the expense of social work status. In those areas which are witnessing both the professionalisation of welfare and the introduction of managerial framework, the social work role is indeed contested. Lewis (1994) highlights UK social workers' feelings of being de-skilled, stressed and undermined as their role shifts from practitioner to co-ordinator. The role of the professional in this general sphere of social welfare is subject to continuing debate and alteration. Work in this area is becoming fragmented, certain tasks are de-professionalised and questions are raised about the further subjugation of vulnerable people through delivering services to them, rather than enabling them to take control of their own welfare. We have then a situation where professionals feel their autonomy is squeezed and where the role of user is changing rapidly.

An additional dimension is that of the professionalisation of management. Traditionally we have seen social workers being supervised by their own, more experienced peers. This has altered to take into account the expanded role of managers. However, one of the founding tenets of managerialism is the belief in the professional manager, the manager who can manage in any context and who does not require either a professional qualification or experience to carry out this role. This belief was fundamental to the Griffiths reviews of health and social services in the 1980s and 1990s in the UK. Whilst we have seen some managers introduced into these spheres without professional backgrounds, this has not been as far reaching as might have been envisaged. This issue constitutes a continuing dilemma. It also reflects the indeterminate nature of career progress within social work. Social workers may seek advancement to their career by moving into management positions to prevent stagnation. Within some social service departments this issue has been addressed by instituting an alternative career route and providing the possibility of further professional advancement to senior practitioner status. Whether this will be acceptable in the longer term remains to be seen. Within the context of developing social work services, other resolutions of this professional-manager tension may be seen as more appropriate. Developments such as these cannot be divorced from the issues of gender identified in earlier chapters.

So we are in a situation which sees the role of professional, of manager and of consumer under considerable scrutiny. A post-modernist view would suggest that the role assigned as 'expert' in social work is changing:

> The professional knowledge of the expert of modernity is based upon the assumption that it is possible to separate true from false by reference to some transcendental standards or guarantees – philosophy, reason, science – as the basis upon which the expert judges and controls those who are subject to the disciplinary gaze (Leonard, 1997, p. 97).

Whilst social work professionals may have been the experts previously the new experts are the managers. This development illustrates the constant realignment and readjustment of the respective rights and responsibilities of each of the above roles in social work organizations. It may be unrealistic to hope for an ideal organisational configuration which accommodates the wishes of each group. We might be better advised to recognise that such re-definitions and re-alignments are necessary and endemic to such a complicated and multi-faceted aspect of human interaction, reflecting also the continuing power struggles of different groups (Leonard, 1997).

The history of social welfare is characterised by a continuing recognition and redefinition of need. Whilst Beveridge provided great inspiration for many in his identification of the 'giants' to attack (the giants of Want, Disease, Ignorance, Squalor and Idleness, see Fraser, 1973), the way in which those giants are defined, let alone attacked, has seen and will continue to see re-definition. In recent years there has been strong pressure to review the concept of need and to attempt to align it with the consumerist notion of demand.

Need and Demand

The change in the role of the recipients of social work and other welfare services has considerable implications for the organisation and delivery of those services. In the past, such recipients were expected to be unquestioning. Need was often defined by statute and identified by bureaucrat or professional. In some of the contexts considered in this book, this is still a predominant position of service users. In contexts such as the UK, the rise of free market philosophies has seen a change in the role of welfare recipient. The words used to define such people are interesting to consider. In post-war social work such recipients were called 'clients', a term undoubtedly adopted in an effort to prevent any stigma which might be attached to being a welfare recipient. The increased emphasis on adopting models and roles from the free market has seen a review of this term which has now moved from client to 'user' and, in some cases, on to 'consumer'. This latter term implies a power in a relationship which is not borne out in practice. The model of social work adopted in most countries is not that of a commercial transaction. Many decisions regarding welfare, as we have seen, are made by agents acting on the behalf of users. Nevertheless, social workers have to accept the concept of 'demand' to some extent. Whereas in a professional or bureaucratic model need would have been defined and imposed, users now, purportedly, have a greater role in defining need in the first instance. This has two sides to it. There has long been a move to include users more integrally in the design and delivery of welfare. To that extent, this new consumerist policy can be seen as a useful means of addressing the power imbalance of the previous model. It enables a more participative approach to welfare. On the other hand, it may imply an unrealistic role for the user. The commercial model suggests an informed and willing consumer. In many cases this does not apply and there are some indications that it is the balance of power between manager and professional, rather than between consumer and professional, which is affected (Klein, 1993).

As with many developments, we can see the positives of the introduction of a new model being offset by difficulties – constant re-definition, constant re-alignment of tensions. Accepting some the difficulties of redefining the user as consumer, this development has caused social work organisations to review the involvement of users and to consider far more than before the issue of standards of quality in care. Not only this, but users are encouraged to feed back into the system comments and criticisms of the service they have received. This is a radical departure from many previous models of state welfare, particular in previously totalitarian regimes. This development contains a further paradox – a consumerist, individualised model of involvement results in greater transparency (of services and standards) and greater accountability of public servants. Recipients of social work services are thus seen as being less dependent and more powerful. However, seeing them only as consumers within a straight, transactional relationship has considerable limitations. Discussion on the roles, rights and responsibilities of citizens in a democracy and as stakeholders in social work organisations needs to develop further.

A further tension endemic in all welfare services is the identification of need at local levels, while resources are largely determined by central mechanisms. However issues of need and demand are addressed, they are influenced considerably by the availability of adequate resources.

From the Simple to the Complex – the Need for Adaptation

Paradox and complexity are evident throughout this book and are highlighted again in this chapter. The greater our experience of social work – both its organization and its delivery, the more complex it appears. At one level this might appear to be somewhat puzzling. However, at another, it is perhaps more understandable. Indeed, Leonard (1997) sees this as being a reflection of the fundamental contradictions which characterise social work, for example, the demand for both care *and* control. If paradox characterises social work, it should be no surprise that its organising mechanisms reflect this. Clarke and Newman (1997), citing some of their own earlier work, argue that we should expect new tensions and contradictions as we attempt to address existing ones:

> Changes of role – from administrators to managers, from controllers to leaders, from client identified 'carers' to resource controllers, from 'professional expert' to provider of services to customers – are likely to lead to a number of dilemmas and tensions, rather than a simple replacement of one role by another (Clarke and Newman, 1997, p. 100).

From the perspectives of postmodernism and poststructuralism, we can see that complexity, diversity, contradiction and paradox do indeed appear to characterise the world of welfare and social work and also that of management and managing. Assumptions associated with previous enlightenment thinking are increasingly questioned (O'Brien and Penna, 1998). Human and social history have been viewed as linear and as demonstrating progress. A fundamentally stable philosophy was seen to underpin development which would lead us towards a unitary world view and a world system which could identify clearly the necessary solutions for a range of social ills. Other philosophical approaches are gaining credence. Poststructuralism advises us to consider the different interpretations which are used in analysing our situation and its intrinsic knowledge and power dynamics. Postmodernism offers us a way of understanding why a modernist view of the world has not provided us with solutions to social problems in all contexts. O'Brien and Penna highlight the complexity resulting from analyses using poststructural and postmodern approaches and their implications:

> The consequence of such complexity is to shift the agenda away from universal prescriptions for alleviating social distress and to emphasise the multiple agenda which any welfare programme generates. In this sense the post-structural critique is central to the debate about the democratisation of welfare and the ways that changing patterns of organization and delivery forge new lines of social inclusion and exclusion (O'Brien and Penna, 1998, p. 132).

In the light of such complexity and acknowledging the many different agendas and means of addressing them, a wide review of welfare approaches is called for. Klein (1993) points to the need to use comparative analysis of different welfare systems in developing greater understanding and adaptability. He suggests that different societal interests and goals are mediated by different political systems. Along with O'Brien and Penna, he recognises that 'generalised theories ... are not helpful in explaining such peculiar patterns (between nations)' (Klein, 1993, p. 15). We need therefore to use theoretical perspectives which acknowledge diverse views. Midgely (1997) also argues for the need for greater global comparisons to be made to enhance both theoretical and professional knowledge which can be applied in practice. To some extent this has been attempted within this book. Klein sees traditional thinking on welfare states as providing some compromise between rampant capitalism on the one hand and centralised communism on the other. Attention should not be devoted to the relative merits of different political systems but to the relative adaptability of the systems and the welfare provision within them.

> not the least important reason why the crisis of the western welfare state was over-predicted, while that of the communist welfare state was under-predicted, was that far too little attention was paid to the respective learning capacity of the two systems (Klein, 1993, p. 15)

Both systems were attempting to manage the tension between maintaining political legitimacy, accumulating capital, regulating expenditure and addressing need. Social welfare services were then designed within particular frameworks. This tension continues: the need for welfare continues. Different frameworks have developed in different local contexts, presenting social work organisations with their own challenges.

This book has attempted to discuss some of the tensions facing social work organisations and their development in different environments. However, the importance of context is not to be diminished. It is from comparison of these different responses in different situations that we gain greater insight into ways in which perennial tensions can be managed. Again this accords with Klein's view:

> diagnosing 'contradiction' i.e. conflicts, in societies does not get us far. Investigating how different societies tackle these conflicts – their institutional capacity for so doing, the structure of power and the

arguments used in the process – is likely to provide far more illumination (Klein, 1993, p. 16).

We have not set out here to provide a normative perspective on social work organisations but to highlight different tensions and different perspectives.

Whilst a postmodern perspective recognises diversity of context and provides further insights on the operation and organisation of social work management, it does have limitations. Indeed, it may present such a view of complexity as to 'disable' analysts from drawing conclusions (Pugh, 1997). Whilst the appreciation of complexity, relativism and diversity is important, there must be some recognition of certain aspects of reality, such as social injustice and oppression, to maintain social coherence. Social coherence and aggregated interpretations of reality are implicit in Leonard's (1997) discussion of the prospect of a future 'emancipatory welfare'. For this to develop there is a need for a new 'solidarity' or recognition of mutual interdependence in economic as well as welfare terms, to enable a localised and responsive 'welfare building' to take place. We must note the variety of discourses which interplay in our current environment and which, if viewed as part of postmodernisation, present us with material for analysis.

What we have seen throughout this book might be viewed as different evolutionary phases in the process of welfare and social work development. What a postmodern perspective encourages us to consider, however, is that we may not be witnessing stages in one evolution but different stages in different evolutions. Mishra (1993) argues that, particularly during 'the Cold War' period, Western welfare states provided an 'alternative social order' (1993, p. 35) to state communism, in addressing need and in serving citizens within a capitalist framework. From a relatively 'steady state' of that era, we have moved to a period of high uncertainty. This social order has changed and will continue to do so. The pre-eminence of the free market economy implies that change is endemic, therefore innovation is essential for continued organizational survival and progress. These themes of change and adaptation in social work organisation and management mirror the same fundamental themes within social work itself (Sheppard, 1995). Within the UK context specifically, Lewis (1994) highlights the impact of such continuing and unpredictable change on social work organisations and on social workers.

Even within one national context, change is not uniform and demonstrates the continuing tensions outlined here and in earlier chapters.

There are many options as to how the tensions are balanced. There is no idealised solution and there is no guarantee that one means of balancing tensions will endure indefinitely. Lewis highlights the difficulties of instituting, adapting to and managing change and the problems that can be caused. These points apply to all who work within social work organisations. Regardless of the time, ingenuity and resources committed to implementation: 'to achieve change is a major challenge but to achieve change without noise may be impossible' (Lewis, 1994, p. 175-6). The challenge for all concerned in social work organisations is to hear the noise but not be deafened by it.

References

Baldock, J. (1994), 'The Personal Social Services: The Politics of Care', in V. George and S. Miller, *Social Policy Towards 2000: Squaring the Welfare Circle*, Routledge, London.
Clarke, J. and Newman, J. (1997), *The Managerial State*, Sage, London.
Fraser, D. (1973), *The Evolution of the British Welfare State*, Macmillan, Basingstoke.
Klein, R. (1993), 'O'Goffe's Tale: or What We Can Learn Form the Success of Capitalist Welfare States', in C. Jones (ed.), *New Perspectives on the Welfare State in Europe*, Routledge, London.
Leonard, P. (1997), *Postmodern Welfare: Reconstructing an Emancipatory Project*, Sage, London.
Lewis, J. (1994), 'Choice, Needs and Enabling: The New Community Care', in A. Oakley and A.S. Williams (eds), *The Politics of the Welfare State*, UCL Press, London.
Midgley, J. (1997), *Social Welfare in Global Context*, Sage, Thousand Oaks, CA.
Mishra, R. (1993), 'Social Policy in a Post-Modern World' in C. Jones (ed.), *New Perspectives on the Welfare State in Europe*, Routledge, London.
O'Brien, M. and Penna, S. (1998), *Theorising Welfare: Enlightenment and Modern Society*, Sage, London.
Parton, N. (1994), 'Problematics of Government: (Post) Modernity and Social Work', *British Journal of Social Work*, vol. 24, pp. 9-32.
Pugh, R. (1997), 'Change in British Social Work: the Lure of Post-modernism and its Pessimistic Conclusions', in B. Lesnik (ed.), *Change in Social Work*, Arena, Aldershot.
Sheppard, M. (1995), *Care Management and the New Social Work: A Critical Analysis*, Whiting and Birch/SCA, London.
Wistow, G., Knapp, M., Hardy, B., Forder, J., Kendall, J. and Manning, R. (1996), *Social Care Markets: Progress and Prospects*, Open University Press, Buckingham.